THE PASSION IN THE GREAT STORY OF JESUS

1. ARREST
2. SANHEDRIN
3. PILATE
4. CROSS
5. DEATH
6. BURIAL

Stephen Joseph Wolf

idjc.org

The Passion in the Great Story of Jesus

Copyright © 2016 Stephen Joseph Wolf
All rights reserved. No part of this book may be copied or reproduced in any
form or by any means, except for the inclusion of brief quotations in a review,
without the written permission of the author or publisher.

Scripture in the Comparative Texts rendered as a study aid in
the present tense and the cover art are by Stephen Joseph Wolf.

The Word of God Proceeded Forth and *Psalm 22* (*O My God, My God, Why Have*)
appeared previously in *Hinge Hour Singer*
and may be treated as in the public domain.

Fragments of Psalms 31 and 69 appeared previously in
One Week in Ordinary Time.

published by idjc press; printed and distributed by Ingram

ISBN 978-1-937081-48-5

Stephen Joseph Wolf is a diocesan parish priest
who spends most Mondays in silence and solitude
writing for faith sharing groups and spiritual direction.

He serves as pastor at
Immaculate Conception Church
in Clarksville, Tennessee.

For information on other faith-sharing titles
see pages 101-103 or visit **idjc.org**.

SOME OF THE VOCABULARY

GREEK	RENDERING	GREEK	RENDERING
Sunedrion	**Sanhedrin**	*doulos*	**slave**
arxierea	**high priest**	*paidiske*	**servant girl**
arxiereis	**chief priests**	*upereton*	**attendants**
irammateis	**scribes**	*Boule*	**council**
presbyteroi	**presbyters,**	*'Ioudaion*	**Judeans**
Pharisaioi	**Pharisees**	*exousian*	**authority**
arxontes	**rulers**	*dynameos*	**power**

THE PASSION IN THE GREAT STORY OF JESUS

A Group Process		4
Possible Group Ground Rules		5
People of the Passion		6
Week 1	**ARREST**	7
	closing: Psalm 22	20
	Map of Jerusalem	22
Week 2	**SANHEDRIN**	23
	closing: Sorrowful Mysteries	
	with the Jesus Prayer	36
Week 3	**PILATE**	39
	closing: Stations of the Cross	54
Week 4	**CROSS**	57
	closing: John Paul II's Stations	70
	North Jerusalem, Looking East	72
Week 5	**DEATH**	73
	closing: Good Friday Reproaches	84
	opening: Suffering Servant Song	86
Week 6	**BURIAL**	87
	closing: verses from the *Stabat Mater*	97
Sources and For More		98

A GROUP PROCESS

This is the simple process I suggest for a 90 minute group meeting:

1. A song that most people know.

2. Some word of God from the Bible.

3. Some Narrative on the Scripture or the theme.

4 Some questions to prompt discussion.

5. A closing prayer to end on time.

For more guidance on leading a group, visit *www.idjc.org*.

Faith sharing with ***The Passion in the Great Story of Jesus*** will be a bit different from other group processes. The focus is on the text. We make the assumption here that the editing done for each of the four gospels has been deliberate. Each gospel, written for a specific community, is God's inspired word for all peoples and decades. We engage these four accounts in the tradition of the Church, and listen for what grabs us and intersects the culture and our own life experience.

Some will want to read this book on their own, and that is normally fine. On this one, gather a handful of friends and read it together.

Blessings,

Rev. Steve Wolf

THE GREAT STORY OF JESUS

POSSIBLE GROUP GROUND RULES

Faith Sharing is:

Regular: I will do my best to make all sessions.

Discerned: There is no need to answer every question. Questions are offered to prompt sharing of stories; it is acceptable to simply offer an observation.

Voluntary: No one is required to share. The tone is invitational; verbal participation is encouraged but not demanded.

Not Interrupted: When someone is sharing, everyone listens before commenting or speaking. Side conversations are avoided, one person at a time.

Not Contradicted: The sharing is based on the person's own life story, so conclusions or critiques of what is shared are not appropriate. Avoid trying to take away feelings with comments like, *You shouldn't feel that way.*

Done in "I" Language: beginning with *I think* or *I feel* rather than *Mary said* or *Joe thinks.*

Confidential: What is said in the group stays in the group.

These ground rules are drawn from Joye Gros' *Theological Reflections,* Loyola Press, 2002, Groups are free to alter them as they wish.

I agree with the group ground rules.   (Signature and Date)

PEOPLE of the PASSION

Annas, former high priest, father-in-law of Caiaphas
Attendants, guards in the temple or for Herod
Barabbas, robber/murderer, literally "son of Abba"
Beloved Disciple, John in the tradition, son of Zebedee
Bystanders, everyday crowd, a multitude
Caiaphas, high priest for 19 years, longest in the 1st century
Centurion, non-Jew giving witness to Jesus
Christ, in Greek: *Anointed One;* in Hebrew: Messiah
Robbers, criminals crucified with Jesus
James & John, sons of Zebedee, in Jesus' inner circle
Jesus of Nazareth, Christ, Son of God and son of Mary
Joseph of Arimathea, member of the Sanhedrin
Judeans, people of Jewish descent and religious practice
Judas, one of the original Twelve Apostles, betrays Jesus
Malchus, high priest's slave, his ear is cut off (by Peter?)
Mary, mother of Jesus, and her sister
Mary Magdalene, disciple of Jesus
Mary (mother of Joses) or another Mary
Nicodemus, member of the Sanhedrin
Peter, in Jesus' inner circle, denies knowing Jesus
Pilate, Roman procurator/governor of Judea
Pilate's Wife, loses sleep over a dream about Jesus
Presbyters, Elders, probably significant lay leaders
Priests, who serve in the Temple
Sanhedrin, the chief priests, scribes, and presbyters
Scribes, experts on the scriptures (Torah/Law)
Simon of Cyrene, forced to help Jesus carry his cross
Soldiers, Roman army or area mercenaries
Women, followers meeting Jesus' needs from Galilee
Young Man, in Mark, runs away from the arrest naked

Week 1
arrest

Opening Prayer: Keep a finger here and join in
the song on the back cover.

← then, take turns reading the "People of the Passion."

Decide together on Faith Sharing Ground Rules, page 5.

> Members of the group read: **Mark 14:32-52**
> *from their personal bibles*,
> one verse at a time, taking turns.
> When it is your turn to read a verse,
> take a silent breath before reading it.
> As each verse is being read aloud,
> other members read along silently . . .

Before going further, let each member of the group name *one* word, phrase, or image that caught his or her attention. Do this *without* any comment or explanation. There is time for that later . . .

☦

Then, take five minutes to review the Passion Narrative Comparative Text on the next seven pages, in silence.

GETHSEMANE (comparative text)

Matthew 26:36-41   Mark 14:32-38

26:30 And having sung a hymn, they go forth to the Mount of Olives.	*14:26 And having sung a hymn, they go forth to the Mount of Olives.*
36 Then Jesus comes with them to a piece of land called <u>Gethsemane</u>,	32 And they come to a piece of land named <u>Gethsemane</u>,
and says to the disciples, "<u>Sit here so going away there I may pray</u>.	and he says to his disciples, "<u>Sit here while I pray</u>."
37 And taking <u>Peter</u> and the <u>two sons of Zebedee </u>he begins to <u>grieve</u> and be <u>distressed</u>; then he says to them, "<u>Deeply grieved is my soul</u>, to death; <u>remain here</u> and <u>watch with me</u>."	33 And he takes Peter and James and John with him, and begins to be <u>greatly astonished</u> and <u>distressed</u>, 34 and says to them, "<u>Deeply grieved is my soul</u>, to death; <u>remain here</u> and <u>watch</u>."
39 And going forward a little he <u>falls on his face</u> praying and saying,	35 And going forward a little he <u>falls to the ground</u>, and prays that if it is possible the hour might pass away from him, 36 and says,
"My Father, <u>if it is possible</u>, <u>let this cup pass</u> from me; <u>yet not as I will but as you</u>."	"<u>Abba</u>, Father, <u>all things are possible to you; remove this cup</u> from me; <u>but not as I wish but as you</u>."
40 And he comes to the disciples and <u>finds them sleeping</u>, and says to Peter, "So were you not able to watch with me one hour? 41 Watch and pray, lest you enter into temptation. <u>Indeed the spirit is eager</u> <u>but the flesh weak</u>."	37 And he comes and <u>finds them sleeping</u>, and says to Peter, "Simon, you sleep? Could you not watch one hour? 38 Watch and pray, Lest you come into temptation; <u>indeed the spirit is eager</u>, <u>but the flesh is weak</u>."

ARREST

GETHSEMANI (comparative text)

Luke 22:39-46   John 18:1

1 Having said these things, Jesus
goes forth with his disciples <u>across the
Kedron Valley</u> where there is <u>a garden</u>

39 And going forth he goes <u>as is
his habit</u> to the <u>Mount of Olives</u>,
and <u>the disciples follow</u> him.

which <u>he and his disciples enter</u>.

40 And coming upon <u>the place</u>
he says to them, "<u>Pray
to not enter into temptation</u>."

41 And he withdraws from them
about a stone's throw
and kneeling he prays asking,
42 "Father, <u>if you will</u>,
<u>take this cup</u> away from me;
<u>but not my will but yours let be</u>."

43 And <u>an angel from heaven</u>
appears to him and strengthens him.
44 And becoming in <u>an agony</u> he prays more earnestly
and <u>his sweat becomes as drops of blood</u>
falling down onto the earth.
45 And rising from prayer, coming to the disciples
he <u>finds them sleeping from the grief</u>, 46 and says to them,
"Why do you sleep? <u>Rise up and pray</u>,
lest you enter into temptation."

THE PASSION IN THE GREAT STORY OF JESUS

BETRAYAL (comparative text)

Matthew 26:42-49

42 Again the second time
going away he prays, saying,
"My Father, if this cannot
pass away except I drink it,
let your will be done."
43 And coming again
he finds them sleeping,
for their eyes are heavy.
44 And leaving them again
going away he prays a third time,
saying again the same words.
45 Then he comes to the disciples
and says to them,
"Sleep now and rest;
Behold: the hour has drawn near
and the Son of humanity is
betrayed into the hands of sinners.
46 Rise; let us go.
Behold: the one betraying me
has drawn near."

47 And while he is still speaking;
Behold: Judas, one of the Twelve
comes, and with him a crowd
with swords and clubs, from
the chief priests and presbyters
of the people.
48 Now the one betraying him
had given them a sign saying,
"Whomever I may kiss, it is he.
Seize him."
49 And immediately
approaching to Jesus, he says,
"Greetings, Rabbi,"
and affectionately kisses him.

Mark 14:39-45

39 And going away again
he prays, saying the same word,

40 And coming again
he finds them sleeping,
for their eyes are becoming heavy,
and they do not know
how they might answer him.

41 And he comes the third time
and says to them,
"Sleep now and rest;
it is enough; the hour has come.
Behold: the Son of humanity is
betrayed into the hands of sinners.
42 Rise; let us go.
Behold: the one betraying me
has drawn near."

43 And immediately while he is
yet speaking, arrives Judas, one of
the Twelve, and with him a crowd
with swords and clubs, from
the chief priests and the scribes
and the presbyters.
44 Now the one betraying him
had given them a signal saying,
"Whomever I may kiss is he.
Seize and lead him securely away."
45 And coming immediately
approaching him he says,
"Rabbi,"
and affectionately kisses him.

ARREST

BETRAYAL (comparative text)

Luke 22:47-48

John 18:2-3

47 While he is <u>speaking,</u>
behold: <u>a crowd</u>, and one of the
twelve, the one named Judas,
comes before them,

2 Now Judas, the one betraying him,
also knows the place, because
Jesus has <u>often assembled there</u>
<u>with his disciples</u>.
3 And so Judas, taking the <u>band of</u>
<u>attendants from the priests and from</u>
<u>the Pharisees</u>, goes there with
<u>lanterns and torches and weapons</u>.

and draws near to Jesus
to kiss him.
48 But Jesus says to him,
"<u>Judas, you betray the Son of</u>
<u>humanity with a kiss?</u>"

THE PASSION IN THE GREAT STORY OF JESUS

ARREST (comparative text)

Matthew 26:50-56

Mark 14:46-52

50 But Jesus says to him,
"Friend, do what you are here to do."
Then approaching they lay their hands
on Jesus and seize him.
51 And behold: one of the ones with
Jesus stretching out his hand draws
his sword, and striking the slave
of the high priest cuts off his ear.
52 Then Jesus says to him,
"Put back your sword into its place;
for all the ones taking a sword
will perish by a sword. Or do you
think that I cannot ask my Father,
and he will provide now for me
more than twelve legions of angels?
How then may be fulfilled the
scriptures that it must be thus?
55 In that hour
Jesus says to the crowds,
"As against a robber you come forth
with swords and clubs to arrest me?
Daily I sat
teaching in the temple,
and you did not seize me.
56 But all this has come to pass
that the scriptures of the prophets
may be fulfilled."
All the disciples leaving him flee.

46 And they lay their hands
on him and seize him.
47 But a certain one of those standing

drawing the sword strikes the slave
of the high priest and cuts off his ear.

48 And answering Jesus says to them,
"As against a robber you come forth
with swords and clubs to arrest me?
49 Daily was I with you
teaching in the temple,
and you did not seize me;
but
that the scriptures
may be fulfilled."
50 And leaving them they all flee.
51 And a certain young man
accompanying him is clothed in
a linen cloth over his nakedness,
and they seize him; 52 and
leaving the linen cloth he flees naked.

ARREST   13

ARREST (comparative text)

Luke 22:49-53   ## John 18:4-11

49 And those around him
seeing the thing happening say,
"Lord, shall we strike
with a sword?"
50 And <u>a certain one of them</u>
strikes the slave of the high priest
and <u>cuts off his right ear</u>.

51 And answering Jesus says,
"<u>No more of this</u>."

And <u>touching the ear he cures him</u>.

52 And Jesus says to the <u>chief</u>
<u>priests and temple guard officers</u>
<u>and presbyters</u> coming upon him,
"<u>As against a robber</u> you come out
with swords and clubs?
53 Daily while I was with you
in the temple you did not
lay your hands against me.
But this is the hour of you
and the <u>authority of darkness</u>."

4 And so Jesus knowing
all the things coming on him
goes forth and says to them,
"<u>Whom do you seek?</u>"
5 They answer him,
"Jesus the Nazarene."
He tells them, "<u>I am</u>."
Now stands also with them
Judas the one betraying him.
6 And so when he tells them "<u>I am</u>,"
<u>they step back and fall to the ground</u>.
7 And so again he questions them,
"Whom do you seek?"
And they say, "Jesus the Nazarene."
8 Jesus answers,
"I told you that I am;
so <u>if you seek me, allow these to go</u>,"
9 that might be fulfilled
the word he said,
"Those whom you have given me,
I lost not one."

10 And so <u>Simon Peter</u>,
having a sword, draws it and
strikes the slave of the high priest
and <u>cuts off his right ear</u>.
The <u>slave's name is Malchus</u>.
11 And so Jesus says to Peter,
"<u>Put the sword into the sheath</u>.
<u>shall I not drink the cup</u> which
my Father has given to me?"

14   ARREST

MATTHEW 26:36-56

J goes to Gethsemane
J takes Peter, James & John
  & prays three times
Judas comes & kisses J
Slave's ear is cut off
J protests his arrest

MARK 14:32-52

J goes to Gethsemane
J takes Peter, James & John;
  & prays three times
Judas comes & kisses J
Slave's ear is cut off
J protests his arrest
Young man flees naked

LUKE 22:39-53

J comes to the place
J withdraws and prays

Judas comes & kisses J
Slave's ear is cut off,
  then cured by J
J protests his arrest

JOHN 18:1-11

J crosses the Kedron
  to a garden

Judas comes, no kiss
Attendants fall
Malchus' right ear is
  cut off by Simon Peter

MARK
*(written about
75 A.D.?)*
↙ ↘

*other Matthew
material*
↓
MATTHEW
*(written about
85 A.D.?)*

*other Lukan
material*
↓
LUKE
*(written about
85 A.D.?)*

↖ ↗

Sayings of Jesus (?)
(lost)

THE PASSION IN THE GREAT STORY OF JESUS

SOME OBSERVATIONS

Most scholars (not all) hold that the Gospel of Mark was written before the others. If we date the passion and resurrection at about 33 A.D., and the editing of what we now call the gospel of Mark at about 75 A.D., there would have been about 40 years when these narratives were likely carried in oral traditions. An early collection of sayings of Jesus (long ago lost if it did exist), called "Q" after the German word for "source," was likely used by the editors of Matthew and Luke. So, the best *theory* is that the editors of Matthew and Luke had in front of them the Gospel of Mark, the "Q" Sayings of Jesus, plus independent traditions and teachings about Jesus. The consensus of the scholars is that John developed from its own tradition, independently of the others, perhaps around 90 A.D.(?).

Jesus knew he was in trouble. His trouble took him to prayer, to the Father. He is also aware that his disciples are in danger. He refers to his suffering as a "cup" to drink. This hearkens to the question to James and John when their mother asked that they be allowed to sit on either side of him in his glory: *Can you drink the cup? You will drink the cup* (Mark 10:38...). All four gospels give us his very human prayer: *If there is another way...* But this prayer is integrated in deep trust: *Your will be done...*

Like Saint Paul's famous *thorn in the flesh* (2 Cor 12:7), the nearest I have come (so far) to Jesus' suffering in Gethsemane has been adult experiences with depression.

16 THE PASSION IN THE GREAT STORY OF JESUS

This is still the closest I have come in describing depression:

> *Everything is heavy.*
> *It takes tremendous effort to get out of a chair.*
> *I eat quite a bit, even more than usual(!),*
> *but nothing tastes very good.*
> *I wake up in the middle of the night,*
> *after a hard time falling asleep.*
> *I do not want to see anyone or talk to friends.*
> *I do not want to exercise or pray.*
> *Movement brings on tears,*
> *so I try to stay very still.*
> *Everything is soggy and excruciatingly heavy.*

This is, best as I can tell, my primary cross. I do not like it; I would not wish it on anyone; nor do I want anyone else's cross. And here is the surprise: I am sometimes grateful for it. The grace of it has been a surprising closeness to God for the stubborn little man called me.

As an old friend likes to quote, comparisons are odious. Still, Gethsemane is a reminder that Jesus knows what it is to suffer, to be aware of it, and to know what it is like to anticipate suffering. Anticipation is sometimes the hardest part. Jesus teaches us to not worry, perhaps because he knows we will. To do so without losing hope, this is his path we follow.

Isn't it strange that when we seem to be at the height of our human powers, especially when we know power in comparison to other people, this is when we

ARREST   17

grow the least in the spirit? Our suffering can take us to
what one of my teachers calls *that deepest place where one is
here and now being created by God:*

> *To pray in the deepest and fullest sense*
> *is to live out of that place,*
> *to immerse oneself in it habitually,*
> *to become at home there.*   Robert Barron

Another great teacher, Fr. Gus Belauskas, celebrating 25
years as a priest, shared from philospher Gabriel Marcel:

> *You feel you are hedged in;*
> *you dream of escape; but beware of mirages.*
> *Do not run or fly away in order to get free: rather,*
> *dig in the narrow place which has been given you;*
> *you will find God there, and everything.*
> *God does not float on your horizon,*
> *he sleeps in your substance.*
> *Vanity runs, love digs.*
> *If you fly away from yourself,*
> *your prison will run with you*
> *and will close in because of the wind of your flight;*
> *If you go deep down into yourself*
> *it will disappear in paradise.*   Gabriel Marcel

This is anything but a peaceful night, but the tired
disciples cannot keep their heavy eyes open. Prayer is not
the place to go to find peace. In prayer, we may meet
everything we fear. As I heard Geshe Sopa put it, *If you
want peace, go to sleep. But if you want to be alive, go to prayer.*
Is it the person about to die who is the most awake?

18 THE PASSION IN THE GREAT STORY OF JESUS

If they knew their eyes were heavy, it was from trying to *stay awake* and *watch*. Prayer is heavy like that sometimes. While wishing that we stay always awake and alert, still Jesus knows what Saint Paul would write, *the Spirit...comes to the aid of our weakness; for we do not know how to pray as we ought, but the Spirit itself intercedes with inexpressible groanings* (Romans 8:26).

In Mark and Matthew, Jesus says, *...see, my betrayer is **at hand*** (or *drawn near*). There is a contrast here with the beginning of Jesus' ministry, where he proclaims, *The kingdom of God is **at hand,*** and then calls the first disciples (Mark 1:15-20). He is still speaking when the betrayer arrives to hand him over. The kiss, a sign of peaceful alliance and friendship, is the method of betrayal in this upside down story.

A Jewish man in a hospital bed once taught me something about the New Testament. He had been told by the Irish Catholic kids in his neighborhood that the death of Jesus was his fault. He always thought that the Christian New Testament used the name *Judas* for the betrayer of Jesus because it sounds similar to the word *Jews.* I shared with him what I had been taught by the Sisters of Mercy, that we ourselves are Judas when we sin. Friendly goodbyes did not quite bridge our worlds.

The use of a sword by Simon (or another) is a sign that disciples are not yet ready for Jesus' cup. Jesus as peacemaker in this situation highlights a saying from one of the Last Supper discourses: *I have much more to tell you, but you cannot bear it now* (John 16:12). What has Jesus said that I might not yet be ready to hear?

ARREST 19

The ear of the high priest's slave is cut off in all four gospels. In John Simon Peter is named as the cutter. What is the symbolism of the cut-off ear? Perhaps: *You're not gonna use it to listen, so you don't need it?* Anyway, Jesus the Healer in Luke restores the lost ear of the slave.

Jesus expresses surprise that he is being treated as an everyday criminal. Though they had to endure the rigamarole with Judas, those with swords and clubs and lanterns still want to pretend that everything is as it should be. What was *normal* was Jesus' *daily* preaching in the temple. They had to do this thing under cover of darkness because, at some honest level, they knew they were acting out of fear. It can be helpful to imagine ourselves in their shoes, as the people with power and responsibility. Then we should keep in mind that almost all of those who were first called by Jesus fled, almost all of them, out of fear. One young man ran away naked! What was that all about? And what about the linen cloth the young man was wearing? Is this baptismal imagery?

ADDITIONAL QUESTIONS

1. Did I notice anything else in the scripture text?

2. How have I acted in anticipation of trouble?

3. Have I had a time of trouble when I was close to God?

4. Our culture usually uses the death penalty right after midnight to not *upset* other prisoners. Why else?

5. Do I respond to violence or being disrespected any differently when I am spending lots of time with God?

THE PASSION IN THE GREAT STORY OF JESUS

CLOSING PRAYER

Are there intercessions from the group?

Psalm 22

O my God, my God, why have you a-ban-doned me?
Why so far from cries for help, rest-less an-guish call?
God, my God/, I call by day, no re-ply to hear.
God, my God, I call by night, no re-lief, I fear.

Yet en-throned, our Ho-ly One God of Is-ra-el,
Trust-ed by an-ces-tors you gave a place to dwell.
They cried out/ to you in need, beg-ging to be free,
Call-ing on their source of hope, free you let them be.

They say I am like a worm, hard-ly hu-man, scorned,
Mocked, de-spised by ev-'ry-one, tar-get of their fun.
All who see/ me mock and scorn, curl their lips and jeer:
"Let your Lord de-liv-er you, save you from your fear."

From the womb you drew me forth, safe-ty at the breast;
From the womb on you I fell, from my birth your guest.
Do not stay/ a-way from me, God, my God since birth;
Near are fear and trou-ble now, help-less I go forth.

Wild/ bulls sur-round a-round, brag-ging on their horns.
Li-ons fierce en-cir-cle me, rend a-bout and roar.
Drain-ing life/ like wa-ter soft, I can bare-ly speak.
Melt-ed is my heart, like wax, all my bones grow weak.

ARREST

Dry as bro-ken bits of pots are my mouth and throat;
Dry tongue stuck in-side my mouth, ta-sting dust and dirt.
I can count/ each of my bones, wa-sted hands and feet;
Pack of dogs close in on me, dogs a-foot com-pete.

At my life they stare and gloat, at my life torn up,
For my clo-thing cast-ing lots, gar-ments rip-ping up.
Save me from/ the li-on mouth, dogs & bulls & sword.
Quick-ly, help, de-liv-er me from this gath-ered hoard.

Then will I pro-claim your name in com-mu-nit-y!
In a-ssem-bly, praise your name, this vow I will keep;
"Ja-cob now/ called Is-ra-el, all de-scen-dants call:
All who fear the Lord, give praise! Hal-le-lu-jah all!

"God did not spurn this one poor soul of mis-er-y,
Did not hide the face from mine, heard my cry in need.
All God's poor/ will eat their fill, all the an-a-wim,
Off-er praise and seek the Lord, hearts a-live in him."

From the edg-es of the earth all will wor-ship God,
Fam-il-ies and na-tions all turn-ing to the Lord.
All king-ship/ be-longs to God, ru-ler of us all.
All the liv-ing and the dead low in hom-age fall.

All who sleep in earth and dust bow in hom-age, kneel.
All de-scen-dants, serve the Lord, live for God, live well.
Tell each gen/-er-a-tion next of the Lord you've known,
Teach de-liv-er-ance to all peo-ple to be born.

Text: from Psalm 22, by Stephen J. Wolf, 2006, tribute to the priesthood of William J. Fleming
Music: 11 11 11 11 ADORO TE DEVOTE, Benedictine Plainsong, Mode V, 13th Century

From *The New Testament of the New American Bible,
Illustrated Saint Joseph Edition with Valuable Study Guide,*
Catholic Book Publishing, New York, 1986, page 14.
Visit catholicbookpublishing.com.

Week 2
sanhedrin

Opening Prayer: Keep a finger here and join in
the Song on the back cover.

Someone reads the Faith Sharing Ground Rules, page 5.

Members of the group read: **Matthew 26:57-27:2**
from their personal bibles,
one verse at a time, taking turns.
When it is your turn to read a verse,
take a silent breath before reading it.
As each verse is being read aloud,
other members read along silently . . .

Before going further, let each member of the group name **one** word, phrase, or image that caught his or her attention. Do this *without* any comment or explanation. There is time for that later . . .

Then, take five minutes to review the Passion Narrative Comparative Text on the next eight pages, in silence.

SANHEDRIN (the text)

Matthew 26:57-58	Mark 14:53-54
57 But the ones <u>seizing</u> Jesus <u>lead him</u> away	53 And they <u>lead</u> Jesus <u>away</u>
to <u>Caiaphas</u> the high priest,	to the <u>high priest</u>, and all the chief priests
where the scribes and presbyters are assembled.	and the presbyters and the scribes come together.
58 And <u>Peter follows</u> him <u>from afar</u>	54 And <u>Peter follows</u> him <u>from afar</u>
<u>up to the court</u> of the high priest, and entering within	until within, <u>in the court</u> of the high priest,
<u>sits with the attendants</u> to see the end.	and <u>sits with the attendants</u> and <u>warms himself by the bright fire</u>.

SANHEDRIN (the text)

Luke 22:54-55

54 And having arrested him,
they <u>lead and bring him</u>
to the <u>house of the high priest</u>,

and <u>Peter follows</u>
<u>from afar</u>.

55 And they light <u>a fire in the</u>
<u>center of the court</u> and sit down
together. Peter <u>sits among them</u>.

In Luke
PETER'S DENIAL
Luke 22:56-62
is properly inserted here.
(see page 29)

John 18:12-18

12 And so the band at the chiliarch
and the attendants of the Judeans
take Jesus and <u>bind him</u>
13 <u>and lead him first to Annas</u>,
for he is the <u>father-in-law of Caiaphas</u>,
who is high priest that year.
14 Now it is <u>Caiaphas</u> who
had <u>advised</u> the Judeans that it is
<u>expedient for one man to die</u>
<u>on behalf of the people</u>.
15 <u>Simon Peter and another disciple</u>
<u>follow Jesus</u>, and that disciple is known
to the high priest and enters with Jesus
into the court of the high priest.
16 But Peter stands <u>outside at the gate</u>.
And so the other disciple known to the
high priest goes and tells the <u>gatekeeper</u>
and <u>brings in Peter</u>.
17 And so the servant-girl gatekeeper
says to Peter,
"<u>Are you not also of the disciples</u>
<u>of this man?</u>"
That one says, "<u>I am not</u>."
18 The slaves and attendants stand
at <u>a fire</u> made because <u>it is cold</u>, and
warm themselves, and Peter also
<u>stands with them and warms himself</u>.

SANHEDRIN (the text)

Matthew 26:59-66

59 And the chief priests and the whole Sanhedrin <u>seek false witness</u> against Jesus <u>that they might put him to death,</u> 60 and do not find any. <u>Many false witnesses</u> do approach.

But later <u>two approach</u>
saying,
"<u>This man said,</u>
 '<u>I can destroy the temple of God</u>
 <u>and after three days build it</u>.' "

62 And standing up
the <u>high priest</u> says to him,
"<u>You answer nothing</u>
 to what these men witness
 against you?"
63 But <u>Jesus remains silent</u>.

And the high priest says to him,
"I order you that by the living God
 you <u>tell us if you are the Christ</u>
 <u>the Son of God</u>."
64 Jesus says to him,
"<u>You say it</u>; yet I tell you, from now
 you will see the <u>Son of humanity</u>
 <u>sitting</u> at the right of the Power and
 coming on the clouds of heaven."
65 Then the high priest
<u>rends his garments</u> saying,
"He <u>blasphemes; what more need</u>
 <u>have we of witnesses?</u>
 Behold: now you hear the <u>blasphemy</u>;
66 what seems it to you?
And answering they say,
"<u>He deserves death</u>."

Mark 14:55-64

55 Now the chief priests and
all the Sanhedrin <u>seek a witness</u>
against Jesus <u>to put him to death,</u>
and <u>find none</u>, 56 though <u>many</u>
<u>witness against him falsely</u>, and
the witnessings are <u>not in agreement</u>.
57 And some standing up witness
against him falsely saying,
"<u>We heard him saying, 'I will</u>
 <u>destroy this handmade temple and</u>
 <u>after three days I will build another</u>
 <u>not made by hands</u>.' " 59 And
their witnessing is not in agreement.
60 And standing up in the midst
the <u>high priest</u> questions Jesus, saying,
"<u>You answer nothing</u>
 to what these men witness
 against you?"
61 But <u>he is silent</u>
<u>and answers nothing</u>.
Again the high priest questions
and says to him,
"<u>You are the Christ,</u>
 <u>the Son of the Blessed One?</u>"
62 And Jesus says,
"<u>I am</u>,
 and you will see the <u>Son of humanity</u>
 <u>sitting</u> at the right of the Power and
 coming with the clouds of heaven."
63 And the high priest
<u>rending his tunics</u>, says,
"<u>What more need</u>
 <u>have we of witnesses?</u>
64 You hear the <u>blasphemy</u>;
 what appears to you?"
And <u>they all condemn him</u>
<u>as deserving death</u>.

SANHEDRIN (the text)

Luke 22:63-71

63 And the men in charge of him
<u>mock and beat him</u>,
64 and <u>blindfold</u> and question him
saying, "<u>Prophesy</u>,
<u>who is the one striking you?</u>"
65 And they say many other things
against him <u>blaspheming</u>.

66 And when day comes,
the presbyters of the people
assemble,
both chief priests and scribes,
and lead him away
to their Sanhedrin, 67 saying,
"<u>If you are the Christ, tell us</u>."
And he says to them,
"<u>If I tell you, you will not believe</u>,
68 and if I question,
you will not answer.
69 But from now the
<u>Son of humanity</u> will be <u>sitting</u>
at the right of the Power of God."
70 And they all say,
"<u>So you are the Son of God?</u>"
And he says to them,
"<u>You say that I am</u>."
71 And they say,
"<u>Why do we need yet more witness?</u>
<u>We ourselves hear from his mouth</u>."

John 18:19-24

19 And so the high priest
questions Jesus about his disciples
and about his teaching.
20 Jesus answers him,
"<u>I have spoken to the world plainly</u>.
I always taught in a synagogue
and in the temple,
where all the Judeans come together,
and <u>I have spoken nothing in secret</u>.
21 Why question me?
Question the ones who heard
what I spoke to them. Behold:
these know what things I said."
22 And as he says these things,
one of the attendants
gives a blow to Jesus, saying,
"Thus you answer the high priest?"
23 Jesus answers him,
"<u>If I speak badly</u>,
<u>witness to the badness;</u>
<u>but if well, why do you beat me?</u>"
24 And so Annas sends him bound
to Caiaphas the high priest.

PETER'S DENIAL (the text)

Matthew 26:67-75

67 Then they <u>spit on his face</u>
and mistreat him with violence,
and they slap him, 68 saying,
"<u>Prophesy to us, Christ</u>:
who strikes you?"

69 And <u>Peter</u> sits outside
in the court and <u>one servant girl</u>
approaches him saying,

"And you were with
Jesus the Galilean."
70 But he denies it before all, saying,
"<u>I do not know
what you say</u>."
71 And going out into the porch
<u>another</u> sees him
and says to the ones there,
"This man was with
Jesus the Nazarene."
72 And <u>again he denies</u>, with an oath,
"<u>I do not know the man</u>."
73 And later ones standing there
approaching say to Peter,
"Truly you are also one of them,
for indeed your speech shows it."
74 Then he begins to curse and swear,
"<u>I do not know the man</u>."
And <u>immediately a cock crows</u>.

75 And Peter remembers
what Jesus said,

"Before a cock crows
you will deny me three times."
And <u>going forth outside</u>
he <u>weeps bitterly</u>.

Mark 14:65-72

65 And some begin <u>to spit at him</u>
and to blindfold his face
and to mistreat him and say to him,
"<u>Prophesy!</u>"
And the attendants with slaps take him.

66 And as <u>Peter</u> is below in the court,
<u>one of the servant girls</u> of the high
priest comes, 67 and seeing Peter
<u>warming himself</u>, looking at him, says,
"And you were with
Jesus the Nazarene."
68 But he denies saying,
"<u>I neither know nor understand
what you say</u>."
And he goes forth outside into
the entry. 69 And <u>the servant girl</u>
sees him and begins again
to say to the ones standing by,
"This man is of them."
70 But <u>he again denies</u>.
And after a little
again the ones standing say to Peter,
"Truly you are of them
indeed for you are a Galilean."
71 And he begins to curse
and to swear,
"<u>I do not know this man you say</u>."
72 And <u>immediately a cock crows
a second time</u>.
And Peter remembers
what Jesus said to him,

"Before a cock crows twice
you will deny me three times."
And he <u>breaks down
and weeps</u>.

SANHEDRIN

PETER'S DENIAL (the text)

Luke 22:56-62
(*out of order*)

John 18:25-27

Luke 22:56-62
PETER'S DENIAL
is inserted here
for comparison.

---

56 And a certain servant girl
seeing him sitting near the light
and gazing at him says,
"And this man was with him."
57 But he denies it saying,
"I do not know him, woman."
58 And after a short while
another seeing him says,
"And you are of them."
But Peter says, "Man, I am not."
59 When about an hour has gone by
another man insists, saying,
"In truth this man was also with him,
 for indeed he is a Galilean."
60 But Peter says,
"Man, I do not know what you say."
And at once while he is yet speaking
a cock crows.
61 And turning
the Lord looks at Peter, and Peter
remembers the word of the Lord,
how he told him that
before a cock crows today
he would deny him three times.
62 And going outside
he weeps bitterly.

25 Now Simon Peter
is standing and warming himself.
And so they say to him,
"Are you not also of his disciples?"
That one denies and says,
"I am not."
26 One of the slaves of the high priest,
a relative of the one
whose ear Peter had cut off, says,
"Did I not see you
 in the garden with him?"
27 Again Peter denies it,

and immediately a cock crows.

SANHEDRIN (the text)

Matthew 27:1-2

1 And when <u>early morning comes</u>, all the chief priests and the presbyters of the people take counsel against Jesus so as to put him to death, 2 and lead him away bound and <u>deliver him to Pilate</u> the governor.

Mark 15:1

1 And immediately at <u>morning</u> in council the chief priests with the presbyters and scribes, all the Sanhedrin, lead Jesus away bound and <u>deliver him to Pilate</u>.

MATHEW 26:57-27:2

J is led to high Caiaphas
   & Peter follows
<u>Sanhedrin night trial</u>
   Temple charge
"Are you the Messiah?"
   Sentence
J is mocked: *Prophesy!*
   Peter's 3 denials
<u>Sanhedrin morning mtg</u>.
J is led to Pilate

MARK 14:53-15:1

J is led to high priest
   & Peter follows
<u>Sanhedrin night trial</u>
   Temple charge
"Are you the Messiah?"
   Sentence
J is mocked: *Prophesy!*
   Peter's 3 denials
<u>Sanhedrin morning mtg</u>.
J is led to Pilate

SOME OBSERVATIONS

The whole thing is accepted in groupthink, because it is *expedient* that one person should die for the people. My dictionary defines the word "expedient" as *suitable for achieving a particular end in a given circumstance; characterized by concern for what is opportune; governed by self-interest.*

SANHEDRIN

31

SANHEDRIN (the text)

Luke 23:1

John 18:28

1 And rising up

28 And so they lead Jesus from Caiaphas <u>to the palace headquarters</u>, and it is early, and <u>they do not enter into the palace headquarters</u> lest they be defiled and thus unable to eat the Passover.

the multitude of them all <u>lead him before Pilate</u>.

LUKE 22:54-23:1

JOHN 18:12-28

J is led to the
 high priest's house
 & Peter follows

Peter's 3 denials
J is mocked: *Prophesy!*
<u>Sanhedrin morning mtg.</u>
"Are you the Messiah?"
J is led to Pilate

J is led to Annas
 & Peter follows
Other disciple admitted
 Peter's 1st denial
<u>Interrogation by the</u>
 <u>high priest</u>
J protests his arrest
Annas sends J to Caiaphas
 Peter's 2nd & 3rd denials
J is led to palace headqtrs.

Look closely at the "transcript." With what crime are they charging Jesus? Is there any solid evidence? If we were in the shoes of the Sanhedrin, might we charge him with any different crime? Would we be able to find more effective false witnesses?

They ask Jesus outright if he is the "*Christ*." A *Messiah* (in Hebrew), *Christ* (in Greek), *Anointed One* (in

English) was expected to come from the family of David as a new king.

Blasphemy is *an insult offered to God in speech,* a violation of the third commandment (Ex 20:7; Deut 5:11) *and is again expressly reproved under pain of stoning* (New World Dictionary).

A second definition of blasphemy is to make oneself equal to God. Perhaps the closest Jesus comes to this is the beginning of his response in Mark to the Messiah question, the words "*I am;...*" God's response to the question of Moses, *Who shall I tell them sent me?,* is God's own name: *YHVH,* meaning *I am,* or *I am who am,* or *I will be who I will be.* So you be a judge: is what Jesus says a blasphemy?

Perhaps as a way to confirm that their judgment is correct, they immediately move from judgment to ridicule. If any prisoner can be made to appear as somehow less than human, not really a child of God but a lunatic or a monster, then anything I do to him or her becomes acceptable. Laughter is a gift meant to give life. Whenever we begin to mock someone, it may say more about our own insecurity than about the nature or virtue of the person scorned. Is this the real reason we dress up prisoners in orange jumpsuits?

Called in all four gospels to follow Jesus, Peter does follow, but at a distance. Only in John's gospel is Peter accompanied by another disciple, strangely by one who is known by the high priest. Peter will deny Jesus, as the Lord predicted. Still we are left asking, where are the others who were also called by Jesus?

SANHEDRIN 33

Remember how Jesus advised his disciples to deal with a brother acting wrongly? First, take it directly to him; then, bring others along to try to persuade him; then, confront him within the community. (See Matthew 18:15-20.) Notice how the maid in Matthew and Mark seems to use this process with Peter, as if she is giving him opportunities to be faithful to Jesus.

How is this for irony: At the Last Supper, Jesus had just served them, washing their feet and teaching them to serve: *If you understand this, blessed are you if you do it* (John 13:17). Of all the people around, it is not a guard or soldier or scribe who gives Peter the opportunity to be faithful. It is a servant. Has God ever seemed to use this kind of irony on you?

Notice also, in John, Peter being confronted by a relative of the very slave to whom Peter had shown violence. All this is happening in the cold. A fire has been built, and all those waiting around want to stay close to the warm fire. The closer Peter goes to the warm fire, the closer he is to light, the more likely they will see his face. And locked up cold inside the palace is the warm mercy of God, captured. Only Luke mentions the Lord turning and looking at Peter. In the three synoptic gospels, we weep with Peter.

This is not the whole story of Peter, but it is an episode with which every disciple of Jesus can identify. Like each of us, the disciple Peter was called by Jesus. Setting side by side the stories of Jesus calling disciples, Simon Peter and all the rest, this is what Jesus looks like in the vocation culture he was building:

Jesus knows our name.

Jesus is a welcoming host.

Jesus gives us a new name.

Jesus knows himself what it is to be called.

Jesus uses us to find and call each other.

Jesus sees our deepest resting places.

Jesus knows his own mysterious name.

Jesus cures to enable hospitality.

Jesus heals to get us ready to hear his call.

Jesus knows his purpose.

Jesus knows what it is to be sent.

Jesus comes to where we live.

Jesus knows where the fish are.

Jesus lifts us up to his purpose.

Jesus takes away all our fear.

As Jesus stands accused, before his own religious leaders, it can be helpful to remember the difference between passivity and pacifism. *Passivity* is about laying down and giving up. *Pacifism* (with the letter *c* like *Pacific*) is rooted in the word *peace*. They are not the same.

The nonviolence which Jesus taught is not about "not struggling;" rather it is about "not using violence." Jesus taught those he called by name to live a kind of provocative, sometimes troublemaking and risk taking nonviolence. In Memphis on April 3, 1968, Martin Luther King, Jr., an outstanding student of the non-violence of Jesus, recollected:

I remember in Birmingham, Alabama, when we were in that majestic struggle there, we would move out of the 16ᵗʰ Street Baptist Church day after day; by the hundreds we would move out. And Bull Connor would tell them to send the dogs forth and they did come; but we just went before the dogs singing, "Ain't gonna let nobody turn me round." Bull Connor next would say, "Turn the fire hoses on." Bull Connor didn't know history. He knew a kind of physics that somehow didn't relate to the transphysics that we knew about. And that was the fact that there was a kind of fire that no water could put out. And we went before the fire hoses; we had known water. If we were Baptist or some other denomination, we had been immersed. If we were Methodist, and some others, we had been sprinkled, but we knew water.

ADDITIONAL QUESTIONS

1. Did I notice anything else in the scripture text?

2. How does Jesus' encounter with the Sanhedrin reflect challenging questions from today's religious leaders, political leaders, employers, media, or others who influence our daily lives?

3. Does anything going on in the world today remind me of the Sanhedrin questioning of Jesus?

4. How might I have denied Jesus? How does my vocation help me to stay faithful?

THE PASSION IN THE GREAT STORY OF JESUS

CLOSING PRAYER

Are there intercessions from the group?

LEADER Let us meditate on the sorrowful mysteries of the rosary of the Blessed Virgin Mary using the *Jesus Prayer* from the Russian Orthodox tradition.

- 1 -

1ST MEMBER *The first sorrowful mystery:*

ALL **The Agony in the Garden.**

1ST MEMBER * *Lord, Jesus Christ, Son of the Living God,*

ALL * **Have mercy on me, a sinner.**

(Repeat, 10 times)

- 2 -

2ND MEMBER *The second sorrowful mystery:*

ALL **The Scourging at the Pillar.**

2ND MEMBER * *Lord, Jesus...*   ALL * **Have mercy...**

- 3 -

3RD MEMBER *The third sorrowful mystery:*

ALL **The Crowning with Thorns.**

3RD MEMBER * *Lord, Jesus...*   ALL * **Have mercy...**

- 4 -

4TH MEMBER *The fourth sorrowful mystery:*

ALL **The Carrying of the Cross.**

4TH MEMBER * *Lord, Jesus...*   ALL * **Have mercy...**

- 5 -

5TH MEMBER *The fifth sorrowful mystery:*

ALL **The Crucifixion and Death.**

5TH MEMBER * *Lord, Jesus...*   ALL * **Have mercy...**

SANHEDRIN

37

Conclude with the *Hail Mary*
and portions of Psalm 69:

Save me, Lord, for waters have come to my neck.
I sink into the deep mire; there is no foothold.
Into deep waters, the floods engulf me.

I am worn out from calling out;
my throat is parched and my eyes fail, looking for my God.

Those hating me for no reason
are more numerous than the hairs of my head.
Many are the ones destroying me
in enmity for no reason.

What I did not steal must I then restore?
You, God, you know my folly
and my faults are not hidden from you.

May those who hope in you, God of Israel,
not be disgraced because of me.
For your sake I endure scorn, and disgrace covers my face.

...You know my scorn and shame and disgrace;
all in enmity are before you.
Scorn broke my heart and I became helpless
and I looked for compassion but there was none,
and for comforters with none to be found.

Instead they put gall in my food
and for my thirst gave me vinegar to drink...

I am in pain and suffering;
may your salvation protect me, O God.   ***Our Father...***

This drawing from the Franciscan Friars of the Holy Land;
donations to them help support Christian Missions in the Holy Land;
contact them at 1400 Quincy Street, Washington, D.C. 20017 or at
www.myfranciscan.org

Week 3
pilate

Opening Prayer: Keep a finger here and join in
the Song on the back cover.

Someone reads the Faith Sharing Ground Rules, page 5.

Members of the group read: **John 18:28-19:16**
from their personal bibles,
one verse at a time, taking turns.
When it is your turn to read a verse,
take a silent breath before reading it.
As each verse is being read aloud,
other members read along silently . . .

Before going further, let each member of the group
name *one* word, phrase, or image that caught his or her
attention. Do this *without* any comment or explanation.
There is time for that later . . .

⊕

Then, take five minutes to review the Passion Narrative
Comparative Text on the next nine pages, in silence.

40 THE PASSION IN THE GREAT STORY OF JESUS

DEATH OF JUDAS (the text)

Matthew 27:3-11a

3 Then <u>Judas, the one who betrayed him</u>, seeing that he is condemned,
repenting returns the <u>thirty pieces of silver</u> to the chief priests and presbyters,
4 saying, "I have sinned, betraying innocent blood."
But they say, "What to us? See to it yourself."
5 And throwing the pieces of silver into the temple, he departs,
and going away <u>hangs himself</u>.
6 But the chief priests take the pieces of silver, saying,
"It is not lawful to put them into the treasury, since it is <u>blood money</u>."
7 So taking counsel they buy with them the <u>field of the potter for burial</u>
<u>for strangers</u>. 8 And so that field is called to this day the <u>Field of Blood</u>.
9 Then is fulfilled as spoken by <u>the prophet Jeremiah</u>,

And they took the thirty pieces of silver,

the price of one with a price, a price set by some sons of Israel,

10 *and gave them for the field of the potter, as the Lord directed me.* (Zech. 11:12-13)

Mark 15:2a

11 And Jesus stands
before the governor; and
the governor questions him, saying, | 2 And Pilate questions him,
"<u>Are you the king of the Judeans?</u>" | "<u>Are you the king of the Judeans?</u>"

NOTE: *'Ioudaion* - **Judeans**
Most translations use the word "Jews." Some scholars suggest these
identifications related to the history of the Temple:
  1. Israelites - during the First Temple, from King Solomon
                to the Babylonian Exile (587 B.C.)
  2. Judeans - during the 2nd Temple, after the Babylonian Exile to 70 A.D.
  3. Jews - Rabbinic Judaism after the destruction of the Second Temple
                    - See John J. Pilch, *The Cultural Dictionary of the Bible,* 1999, pp. 99-101

PILATE   41

PILATE (the text)

John 18:29-37a

29 And so <u>Pilate</u> goes forth outside
to them and says,
"<u>What accusation</u>
do you bring of this man?"
30 They answer and say to him,
"<u>If this man was not doing badness</u>
<u>we would not deliver him to you</u>."
31 And so Pilate says to them,
"You take him and judge him
according to your law."
The Judeans say to him,
"<u>It is not lawful for us to kill anyone</u>,"
32 this that the word spoken by Jesus
might be fulfilled signifying
the death by which he would die.

Luke 23:2-3a

2 And they begin to accuse him,
saying, "<u>We found this man</u>
<u>distressing our nation and opposing</u>
<u>paying taxes to Caesar,</u> and
<u>saying himself to be Christ, a king</u>."
3 And Pilate questions him, saying,
"<u>Are you the king of the Judeans?</u>"

33 And so Pilate enters again
into the palace headquarters
and calls Jesus and says to him,
"<u>Are you the king of the Judeans?</u>"
34 Jesus answers,
"<u>Do you say this from yourself,</u>
<u>or have others told you about me?</u>"

35 Pilate answers,
"I am not a Judean, am I? Your people and the chief priests
delivered you to me. What did you do?"
36 Jesus answers,
"My kingdom is not of this world; if my kingdom was of
this world my attendants would be fighting that I not be
delivered to the Judeans. But <u>my kingdom is not now here</u>."
37 And so Pilate says to him,
"Are you not really a king?"

PILATE (the text)

Matthew 27:11b-14

And Jesus says,
"You say it."

12 And as he is accused by
the chief priests and presbyters,
he answers nothing.
13 Then Pilate says to him,
"Do you not hear
the things
they give witness against you?"
14 And he does not answer him,
not one word, so that
the governor is astonished
exceedingly.

Mark 15:2b-5

And answering him he says,
"You say it."

3 And the chief priests
accuse him of many things.
4 But Pilate again questions him,
saying,
"Do you not answer anything?
Behold: of how many things
they accuse you."
5 But Jesus answers nothing more,
so that
Pilate is astonished.

PILATE

PILATE (the text)

Luke 23:3b-12

And answering him he says,
"<u>You say it</u>."

4 And Pilate says to the
chief priests and the crowds,
"<u>I find no crime in this man</u>."
5 But they insist saying,
"<u>He stirs up the people</u>,
teaching through all Judea,
<u>beginning in Galilee, even to here</u>."

6 And Pilate hearing, questions if the man is <u>a Galilean</u>;
7 and learning that he is of <u>Herod's jurisdiction</u>,
he sends him up to Herod, being also in Jerusalem in these days.
8 And seeing Jesus, <u>Herod rejoices greatly</u>;
for he has <u>been wishing for a long time to see him</u>
because he has heard about him
and he hopes to see some sign done by him.
9 And he <u>questions him in many words</u>
but <u>he answers him nothing</u>.
10 And the chief priests and the scribes
stand and vehemently accuse him.
11 And <u>despising and mocking him</u>,
Herod and his soldiers
<u>dress him up in splendid clothes</u>
and <u>send him back to Pilate</u>.

12 And <u>Herod and Pilate</u>
<u>became friends with each other</u>
<u>on this same day</u>,
for they had been in enmity.

John 18:37b-38

Jesus says,
"<u>You say that I am a king</u>.
I was born for this, and
<u>for this I have come into the world</u>,
<u>that I might witness to the truth</u>.
Everyone being of the truth
hears my voice."
38 Pilate says to him,
"<u>What is truth?</u>"
Having said this he goes forth again
to the Judeans, and tells them,
"<u>I find no crime in him</u>."

THE PASSION IN THE GREAT STORY OF JESUS

PILATE (the text)

Matthew 27:15-23

15 Now <u>at a feast</u> the governor is
<u>accustomed</u> to release to the crowd
one prisoner whom they wish.
16 And they have a
<u>notorious prisoner</u> named <u>Barabbas</u>.

17 When they are assembled,
Pilate says to them,
"Whom do you wish
 I may release to you,
 Barabbas or Jesus called Christ?"
18 For <u>he knows</u> that they
deliver him because of <u>envy</u>.
19 Now as he sits on the judge-seat,
his <u>wife sends to him</u> saying,
"<u>Do nothing with that just man,</u>
 <u>for I suffer many things today</u>
because of <u>a dream of him</u>."
20 But the <u>chief priests and the</u>
<u>presbyters persuade the crowds</u>
that they should <u>ask for Barabbas</u>
and should <u>destroy Jesus</u>.
21 So answering
the governor says to them,
"Which one from the two do you
 wish I may release to you?"
And they say, "Barabbas."
22 And Pilate says to them,
"What then may I do
 to <u>Jesus called Christ</u>?"
They all say,
"<u>Let him be crucified</u>."
23 But he says,
"Why? <u>What bad thing did he do?</u>"
But they cry out more, saying,
"<u>Let him be crucified</u>."

Mark 15:6-14

6 Now <u>at a feast</u>
<u>he would</u> release to them
one prisoner whom they requested.
7 Now there is the one named
<u>Barabbas</u>, bound with the rebels,
who <u>in the rebellion had done murder</u>.
8 And the crowd going up begins to
ask for what he used to do for them.
9 But Pilate answers them saying,
"Do you wish that I may release to you
 the king of the Judeans?"
10 For <u>he knows</u> the chief priests
deliver him on account of <u>envy</u>.

11 But <u>the chief priests</u>
<u>stir up the crowd</u> that he should
<u>rather release</u> to them <u>Barabbas</u>.

12 So Pilate again answering
says to them,
"What then may I do to <u>him whom</u>
 <u>you call the king of the Judeans</u>?"
13 And they again cry out,
"<u>Crucify him</u>."
14 But Pilate says to them,
"Why? <u>What bad thing did he do?</u>"
And they cry out more,
"<u>Crucify him</u>."

PILATE   45

PILATE (the text)

Luke 23:13-23

13 And <u>calling together the chief
priests, the rulers, and the people,</u>
Pilate 14 says to them,
"<u>You brought me this man</u> as
upsetting the people, and behold:
examining before you, I find in this
man nothing of what you accuse him.
15 Nor does Herod, for he sends
him back to us. And behold:
<u>nothing worthy of death has been
done by him.</u> 16 So <u>I will have him
flogged and released</u>."

(verse 17 is omitted)

18 But they shout with the
whole multitude saying,
"<u>Take this man</u>
and <u>release to us Barabbas</u>,"
who had been <u>thrown into prison</u>
because of a <u>rebellion</u> in the city
and <u>murder</u>.

20 But wishing to release Jesus,
Pilate again calls to them.
21 But they shout saying,
"<u>Crucify! Crucify him!</u>"
22 But he says to them a third time,
"But <u>what bad thing did this man do?
I find no cause for death in him.
So I will have him flogged
and released</u>."

23 But they insist with <u>loud voices</u>
that he be crucified,
and <u>their voices prevail</u>.

John 18:39 - 19:7

39 But you have a <u>custom</u> that I should
release one to you <u>at the Passover</u>.
So do you will that I release to you
the <u>king of the Judeans</u>?"
40 And so they cry out again saying,
"Not this man, but Barabbas."
But <u>Barabbas was a robber</u>.

1 And so Pilate takes Jesus and
<u>scourges him</u>. 2 And the <u>soldiers
twisting a crown out of thorns</u>
put it on his head 3 and throw
a <u>purple garment</u> around him,
and come to him and say,
"<u>Greetings, king of the Judeans</u>,"
and they <u>give him blows</u>.

4 And Pilate again goes forth outside
and says to them,
"Behold: I bring him out to you,
that you may know that
<u>I find no crime in him</u>."
5 And so Jesus comes forth outside
<u>wearing the crown of thorns and the
purple garment</u>. And he says to them,
"<u>Behold: the man</u>."
6 And so when the chief priests and
the attendants see him,
They shout, saying,
"<u>Crucify! Crucify!</u>"
Pilate says to them,
"<u>You take him and crucify,
for I find no crime in him</u>."
7 The Judeans answer him,
"We have a law, and <u>according to
the law he ought to die because
he made himself Son of God</u>."

PILATE (the text)

Matthew 27:24-26 Mark 15:15

Matthew 27:24-26	Mark 15:15
24 And seeing that nothing is gained but rather an uproar is occurring, <u>taking water Pilate washes his hands</u> in front of the crowd saying, "<u>I am innocent of this man's blood;</u> <u>see to it yourselves</u>." 25 And answering all the people say, "His blood be on us and on our children." 26 Then he releases Barabbas to them.	15 And Pilate resolving to satisfy the crowd

releases Barabbas to them, |
| But Jesus, having him scourged, he delivers that he might be crucified. | and delivers Jesus, having him scourged, that he might be crucified. |

PILATE

47

PILATE (the text)

Luke 23:24-25

John 19:8-16

24 And Pilate decides to
carry out their request,

25 and he releases the one
thrown into prison because
of rebellion and murder;

8 And so when Pilate hears this word,
he is more afraid, 9 and enters again
into the palace headquarters
and says to Jesus,
"Where are you from?"
But Jesus gives him no answer.
10 And so Pilate says to him,
"Do you not speak to me? Do you know that
I have authority to release you and I have
authority to crucify you?"
11 Jesus answers,
"You have no authority over me unless it is
given you from above. And so the one who
has delivered me to you has a greater sin."
12 From this Pilate seeks to release
him, but the Judeans shout saying,
"If you release this man,
you are not a friend of Caesar.
Everyone making himself a king
speaks against Caesar."
13 And so Pilate hearing these words
brings Jesus outside and sits on a judge-
seat in a place called Stone Pavement,
in Hebrew Gabbatha.
14 Now it is Preparation Day of the
Passover, at about the sixth hour,
and he says to the Judeans,
"Behold: your king."
15 And so those shout,
"Take, take, crucify him!"
Pilate says to them,
"Shall I crucify your king?"
The chief priests answer,
"We have not a king except Caesar."
16 And so he then delivers him to
them that he might be crucified.

but he delivers Jesus
to their will

THE PASSION IN THE GREAT STORY OF JESUS

MATTHEW 27:3-26
Death of Judas
"King of the Jews?"
Barabbas
J is scourged
Pilate washes his hands
J is sentenced to cross

MARK 15:2-15

"King of the Jews?"
Barabbas
J is scourged

J is sentenced to cross

LUKE 23:2-25
Accusations
"King of the Jews?"
Pilate: *no crime*
J is sent to Herod, mocked
J is returned to Pilate
Barabbas

J is delivered to them

JOHN 18:29-19:16
What accusation?
"King of the Jews?"
Pilate: *no case*
Barabbas
J is scourged, mocked
"Behold the man"
Pilate is challenged by J
"Here is your king"
J is handed to them to
be crucified

SOME OBSERVATIONS

Thirty pieces of silver is the compensation due to a slaveowner whose slave has been gored by an ox. Thirty pieces of silver is used in the allegory of the prophet Zechariah as the good shepherd who has been treated badly by the sheep owners. Thirty pieces of silver is thus meant to be understood as a cheap price, a symbol of contempt. (Exodus 21:32; Zechariah 11:13) The thirty pieces are mentioned only in Matthew.

PILATE

49

The other account of the death of Judas is in the Book of Acts (1:18-19): *He bought a parcel of land with the wages of his iniquity, and falling headlong, he burst open in the middle, and all his insides spilled out.* Yuck. And Acts does not mention Judas being aware of having done wrong, clearly stated in Matthew, where his confession is made to the same religious leaders who paid him for his betrayal, and their response is *"What is it to us?"*

Among the saints, only Mary is named in our Nicene Creed. So is Pontius Pilate, Prefect of Judea from 26 to 36 A.D., in the years of the ministry of the Baptist and Jesus.

> To Pilate's credit is the building of an aqueduct from Bethlehem to Jerusalem which provided the capital and the Temple for the first time with an ample water supply for all contingencies. Pilate is accused of weakness of character (in all four Gospels: Mt 27:11-26; Mk 15:1-15; Lk 23:1-25; Jn 18:29-19:17). Perhaps his action is better explained by the two motifs of his rule: on the one hand his complete inability to understand the Jews and everything Jewish, and on the other the determination not to compromise his position as prefect which was already endangered by repeated complaints of the Jews (see Jn 19:12). His shaky standing in Rome probably explains why Herod Antipas wanted no part of a decision Pilate had to make (Luke 23:12). Summoned to Rome to answer to Tiberius, the new emperor Caligula retired Pilate without other penalty. Stories of his fate are but legends; he slips out of history.
>
> *New World Dictionary Concordance to the New American Bible*

THE PASSION IN THE GREAT STORY OF JESUS

John's gospel implies from the beginning that Pilate wants no part of the Jesus controversy. He agrees to consider the matter only after the religious leaders admit that the law of the state places him in a status above theirs, quite an admission.

The big question: *"Are you the king of the Jews?"* is the question everyone wants answered. *King of the Jews* is a name for Jesus used only by pagans such as Pilate.

"You have said so" (Revised Standard Version) or *"You say so"* (New American Bible) in Matthew, Mark and in Luke, are the final words Jesus has for Pilate. Perhaps Jesus withholds an unqualified *"yes"* because the kingship Jesus has in mind is not what Pilate would understand it to be. *"You have said so"* is also Jesus' response to the question of Judas at the Last Supper, *"Surely it is not I, Rabbi?"*

When Jesus answers Pilate (in John), *"Do you say this of your own accord...?,"* does it suggest a willingness to engage even Pilate as a potential disciple? Have you ever met a more gutsy salesperson? Jesus does try to make clear to Pilate that Jesus is king of a kingdom different from any Pilate has ever known.

All that Jesus says then leads Pilate to that great question for all times, *"What is truth?"* The truth is standing in front of Pilate, who goes to the religious leaders and reports he finds no crime in Jesus. In Matthew and Mark, Jesus' non-response leaves Pilate astonished. Know the feeling? Our faith is so bold as to say that in the person of Jesus Christ, God has said everything that God wishes to say about who God is and who we are called to be. Worthy indeed of wonder.

PILATE

51

Pilate's problem is the practical situation of a troublemaker who *"stirs up the people,"* from Galilee to Jerusalem. Galilee! A spark, perhaps a way out for Pilate. Jesus is a Galilean, so let Herod deal with it.

Only in Luke is Jesus sent to Herod (Antipas), the one who ordered John the Baptist beheaded. This Herod's father, "Herod the Great," was the Herod of early Luke, responsible for the Bethlehem slaughtering of the innocent boys two years old and younger. This son of Herod the Great is fascinated with Jesus, but gets no answers to his questions. In the end, Herod treats Jesus with contempt. In Luke, the enemies, Herod and Pilate, forge the classic new friendship of scoundrels.

"Barabbas" is an Aramaic name meaning "son of the father." Get the irony of the choice Pilate offers to the people? The "custom" of the feast is mentioned in all of the gospels except Luke. *Outside of the gospels there is no direct attestation of it, and scholars are divided in their judgment of the historical reliability of the claim that there is such a practice* (New American Bible footnote to Mt 27:15). John mentions Barabbas in one economical verse: John 18:40.

In Matthew and Mark and John, we are told of Jesus being scourged. The scourging is to weaken the victim and so hasten the coming of death. The whips of leather would hold hard pieces of metal or bone. This event was used for long drama in the movie *The Passion of Christ*. As we grow closer to Jesus, does this scene become more difficult to bear?

In a drawing by a Franciscan, Jesus is standing bound before Pilate, who is kind of playing with a knife.

He is in control; that is the message. He has power. Of course, if someone has the power to put someone to death, he or she also has the power to set them free. The power can prod him out toward the cross. Power can also cut the ties that bind him. This burden of leadership and power is huge, shared by today's governors and presidents in the common law practice of the pardon.

Jesus is mocked outright and in symbolic ways: the crowd choosing a known criminal, Pilate allowing them to release a known insurrectionist, clothing him in royal colors, etc. Perhaps the worst insult is when the chief priests say out loud, *"We have no king but Caesar!"* What a scandal if a child heard them say this. It is one thing to deny Jesus; it is another to deny their own God. Only in Matthew does Pilate wash his hands, the action most often used by artists to portray him.

Serving one summer as a hospital chaplain gave some rich experiences with chaplains of other faiths and denominations. One powerful afternoon, a delightful Baptist chaplain broke out in a gospel song:

> *Everybody ain't able.   Everybody ain't able.*
> *__EV__'rybody ain't able… to be\ a fooool.*

Jesus is stripped, beaten, mocked, crowned, robed, laughed at, derided, made fun of, treated like a fool. When we too have to be a "fool for Christ," it can be so helpful to remember that in this way too, we are imitating him.

St. Ignatius of Loyola names in his *Spiritual Exercises* three degrees of humility:

PILATE

1. Avoiding Serious Sin - a basic commitment
2. Avoiding little sins - the small things
3. Accepting rejection/defeat in union with Jesus.

Really? Accepting rejection and suffering, defeat and ridicule? Yes, in union with Christ; in awareness of God's complete love. As one spiritual director puts it:

a) Accept it.
b) Expect it   (not looking for it, but nor being surprised when it comes).
c) Almost savor it.   (This is what St. Paul did.)

In Jesus, God has given us the **concrete form** in which God's reign on earth is to be established. Jesus comes as Savior in a world broken by human autonomy: self-assertion, exploitation, self-righteousness. Jesus' message was rejected in his time, and so it will be rejected also today. Jesus had no weapons, material resources, or social or political power. Jesus had only the good news of God's reign.

We too have to learn to not rely on institutional power. This path will be hard to follow. Jesus too prayed to not suffer, not die. No one expects us to love pain and death. Still, we know that in suffering we are close to Jesus, similar to him, united with his saving passion as his true disciples.

There is an ultimate norm for our decisions: God has spoken in Jesus, his Son. His life of love, his struggle against injustice and sin, his rejection and his passion are the model in which we, his disciples, see our life and mission.

Spiritual Exercises of Saint Ignatius of Loyola, #165-168
drawn from the version given by Rev. Peter Bahi, SJ, on my 30-day retreat

54 THE PASSION IN THE GREAT STORY OF JESUS

ADDITIONAL QUESTIONS

1. Did I notice anything else in the scripture text?

2. Does the trial before Pilate have anything to say about the controversies growing out of the murky relationship between church and state?

3. What role does "truth" play in my life?

4. Can I think of any figure in art, film or literature who might be rooted in the artist or writer's understanding of Pilate or Jesus?

CLOSING PRAYER

Are there intercessions from the group?

then continue with the
STATIONS OF THE CROSS
(adapted from *Breaking Bread 2006* hymnal)
Group members take turns leading.

1st Jesus is condemned to death;
Christ, give us the wisdom to seek the Father's will.
OUR FATHER...

2nd Jesus bears his cross;
Lord, help us each to name our cross and to pick it up daily.
HAIL MARY...

3rd Jesus falls for the first time;
Christ, show us how to rely on your strength when we fail.
GLORY BE...

4th Jesus meets his mother;

Lord, hear your mother praying that we be consoled.

OUR FATHER...

5th Jesus is helped by Simon;

Christ, empower us to do your work in the world.

HAIL MARY...

6th Veronica wipes his face;

Lord, prompt us to be your assisting hand for those in need.

GLORY BE...

7th Jesus falls the second time;

Christ, take us to the healing power of penance.

OUR FATHER...

8th Jesus speaks to the women;

Lord, let us be a comfort those in anxiety.

HAIL MARY...

9th Jesus falls a third time;

Christ, bless us with the grace to persevere.

GLORY BE...

10th Jesus is stripped of his garments;

Lord, help us to follow you in honest humility.

OUR FATHER...

11th Jesus is nailed to the cross;

Christ, draw us closer to you when we are wounded.

HAIL MARY...

12th Jesus dies on the cross;

Lord, we pray, be with us at the hour of our death.

GLORY BE...

13th He is taken from the cross;

Christ, open our hearts to the beauty of your tender love.

OUR FATHER...

14th He is laid in the tomb;

*Lord, keep us each faithful on our day
of following you through death to life.* HAIL MARY...

Week 4

cross

Opening Prayer: Keep a finger here and join in the Song on the back cover.

Someone reads the Faith Sharing Ground Rules, page 5.

>Members of the group read: **Luke 23:26-43** *from their personal bibles*, one verse at a time, taking turns. When it is your turn to read a verse, take a silent breath before reading it. As each verse is being read aloud, other members read along silently . . .

Before going further, let each member of the group name *one* word, phrase, or image that caught his or her attention. Do this *without* any comment or explanation. There is time for that later . . .

Then, take five minutes to review the Passion Narrative Comparative Text on the next five pages, in silence.

THE PASSION IN THE GREAT STORY OF JESUS

MOCKERY BY SOLDIERS (the text)

Matthew 27:27-33

Mark 15:16-22

27 Then the governor's soldiers
take Jesus
into the <u>palace headquarters</u>
and assemble against him
<u>all the cohort</u>.
28 And <u>stripping him</u> they place
around him a <u>scarlet cloak</u>,
29 and having <u>twisted</u>
a <u>crown of thorns</u>
they place it on his head
and a <u>reed</u> in his right hand, and
<u>bending the knee</u> in front of him
<u>mock him</u> saying,
"<u>Greetings, King of the Judeans</u>,"
30 and spitting at him
take the reed and strike at his head.

31 And when they have mocked him,
they strip him of the cloak
and put his garments on him.

16 Then the soldiers
lead him away inside the court
of the governor's <u>palace headquarters</u>,
and they call together
<u>all the cohort</u>.

17 And they put on him a <u>purple robe</u>
and place <u>twisting around him</u>
a <u>crown of thorns</u>.

18 And they begin to <u>salute him</u>,
"<u>Greetings, King of the Judeans</u>."
19 And they <u>strike his head</u>
<u>with a reed</u> and spit at him,
and <u>bending their knees worship him</u>.
20 And when they have mocked him
they strip him of the purple robe
and put his garments on him.

They <u>lead him away</u>
to crucify him.
32 And going forth they find <u>a man</u>,
A <u>Cyrenian named Simon</u>;
they <u>force</u> this man

to take up his cross.

21 And they <u>lead him forth</u>
that they might crucify him.
And they <u>compel</u> <u>passing by</u>
a certain <u>Simon, a Cyrenian</u>
coming <u>from the country</u>,
the <u>father of Alexander and of Rufus</u>,
that he might take up his cross.

33 And coming to <u>a place</u>
<u>called Golgotha</u>, which is called
a Place of a Skull,

22 And they bring to <u>the place</u>
<u>Golgotha</u>, meaning
Place of a Skull.

CROSS   59

WAY OF THE CROSS (the text)

Luke 23:26-33a   John 19:17

26 And as they <u>lead him away</u>,
<u>seizing</u> Simon, <u>a certain Cyrenian</u>
<u>coming from the country</u>,
they <u>place on him the cross</u>
to carry <u>behind Jesus</u>.

27 And following him is <u>a multitude</u>
of the people and of <u>women</u>
who mourn and lament him.
28 And turning to them Jesus says,
"<u>Daughters of Jerusalem</u>,
<u>do not weep over me</u>,
<u>but weep over yourselves</u>
<u>and over your children</u>,
29 because behold: days are
coming when they will say,
'Blessed are the barren and
the wombs which do not bear,   And so they take Jesus,
and breasts which never nurse.'   17 and <u>carrying the cross to himself</u>
30 Then they will begin to say
to the mountains, 'Fall on us,'
and to the hills, 'Cover us,'
31 <u>for if a tree in full sap</u>
<u>they do these things</u>,
<u>what may happen in the dry?</u>"

32 And led with him are
<u>two criminals</u> to be killed.   he goes forth
                                      to <u>what is called</u>
33 And when they come upon   <u>Skull Place</u>, which is called
the <u>place called Skull</u>,   in Hebrew <u>Golgotha</u>.

CRUCIFIXION (the text)

Matthew 27:34-44　　　Mark 15:23-32

34 they give him
wine mixed with gall to drink;
and tasting he would not drink.
35 And having crucified him they
divide his garments, casting a lot,
36 and sitting there they guard him.
37 And they place above his head
his accusation, inscribed,
"THIS IS JESUS
THE KING OF THE JUDEANS."
38 Then two robbers are crucified
with him, one on the right
and one on the left.
39 And the passersby blaspheme him,
wagging their heads 40 and saying,
"The one destroying the temple
 and building it in three days,
 save yourself, if you are Son of God,
 and come down from the cross."
41 Likewise also the chief priests,
mocking with the scribes and
presbyters, say,
42 "Others he saved,
 himself he cannot save;
 he is King of Israel,
 let him come down now from the
 cross and we will believe on him.
43 He has trusted on God,
 let him rescue now if he wants him.
 for he said, "I am Son of God."
44 And also the robbers
crucified with him
heap the same insults on him.

23 And they give him
wine spiced with myrrh,
but he does not take it.
24 And they crucify him
and divide his garments, casting a lot
on which one might take them.
25 Now it is the third hour *(9 am)*
when they crucify him. 26 And the
accusation is inscribed above him:
"THE KING OF THE JUDEANS."
27 And with him they crucify
two robbers, one on his right
and one on his left.
29 And passersby blaspheme him
wagging their heads and saying,
"Ah, the one destroying the temple
 and building it in three days,
30 save yourself
 coming down from the cross."
31 Likewise also the chief priests
mocking to one another with
the scribes say,
"He saved others;
 himself he cannot save;
32 the Christ, the King of Israel,
 come down now from the cross,
 that we may see and believe."

And the ones
crucified with him
heap insults on him.

CROSS

61

CRUCIFIXION (the text)

Luke 23:33b-43

there <u>they crucify him</u>
and the <u>criminals</u>,
one on the <u>right</u> and one on the <u>left</u>.
34 And Jesus says,
"<u>Father, forgive them; for they
know not what they do</u>."
And <u>dividing his garments</u> <u>they cast
lots</u>. 35 And beholding, <u>the people
stand and scoff</u> and <u>with the rulers</u> say,
"He saved others; <u>let him save himself</u>
if this man is the Christ of God,
the chosen one."
36 And the soldiers also approach
and mock him, offering him <u>vinegar</u>
37 and saying, "If you are the King
of the Judeans, <u>save yourself</u>."
38 And there is also an inscription
over him: "<u>THIS IS
THE KING OF THE JUDEANS</u>."
39 And <u>one of the criminals</u> hung
blasphemes him,
"Are you not the Christ?
Save yourself and us."
40 But <u>answering</u>
<u>the other</u> rebukes him saying,
"Do you not fear God? You are
under the same judgment, 41 and
we indeed justly, for things worthy
of what we did we receive back;
<u>but this man did nothing wrong</u>."
42 And he says,
"<u>Jesus, remember me
when you come into your kingdom</u>."
43 And he says to him,
"Amen I tell you, <u>today you will be
with me in the Paradise</u>."

John 19:18-27

18 There they crucify him, and with
him <u>two others</u>, <u>on this side and on that</u>
and <u>Jesus in the middle</u>.
19 And Pilate writes a title and puts it
on the cross, having written,
"<u>JESUS OF NAZARETH
THE KING OF THE JUDEANS</u>."
20 And so many of the Judeans read
this title, because the place where Jesus
is crucified is near the city. And it is
written in <u>Hebrew</u>, in <u>Latin</u>, and in
<u>Greek</u>. 21 And so the chief priests
of the Judeans say to Pilate,
"Do not write, 'King of the Judeans,'
but '<u>that man said, I am king of the
Judeans</u>.'"   22 Pilate answers,
"<u>What I have written, I have written</u>."
23 And so when they crucify Jesus the
soldiers take <u>his garments</u> and <u>make
four parts, a part to each soldier</u>, and
the tunic. Now the <u>tunic</u> is <u>seamless</u>,
from the top <u>woven throughout</u>.
24 And so they say to one another,
"Let's not tear it, but let's
<u>cast lots</u> over whose it shall be,"
that the scripture might be fulfilled,
*They divied up my garments among them-
selves, and over my clothing they cast a lot,*
and so the soldiers do these things.
25 But <u>standing there by the cross</u> of
Jesus is <u>his mother</u> and <u>the sister of his
mother</u>, <u>Mary of Clopas</u>, and <u>Mary the
Magdalene</u>. 26 And so Jesus seeing his
mother and standing by <u>the disciple
whom he loves</u>, says to his mother,
"<u>Woman, behold: your son</u>."
27 Then he says to the disciple,
"<u>Behold: your mother</u>." And from that
hour the disciple takes her to his own.

THE PASSION IN THE GREAT STORY OF JESUS

MATTHEW 27:27-44

Soldiers mock J
Simon of Cyrene
Comes to Golgotha (Skull)
Wine with gall
Crucify him
Lots for garments
Inscription over him
Robber on each side
Passersby deride J
Priests & Scribes mock
Co-crucified revile J

MARK 15:16-32

Soldiers mock J
Simon of Cyrene
Comes to Golgotha (Skull)
Wine with myrrh
Crucify him
Lots for garments
Inscription over him
Robber on each side
Passersby deride J
Priests & Scribes mock
Robbers revile J

LUKE 23:26-43

Simon of Cyrene
Daughters of Jerusalem
Comes to Skull
Crucify him
Criminal on each side
"Father, forgive them..."
Lots for garments

People watch him
Rulers scoff
Soldiers mock J
Vinegar is offered
Inscription over him
One criminal reviles J;
   other defends him
"This day in Paradise..."

JOHN 19:17-27

J carries his own cross

Comes to Golgotha (Skull)
Crucify him
Another one on each side
Cross title challenge
Priests vs. Pilate
Garments divided by 4
Lots for the tunic
Mary the mother
Sister of Mary
Mary of Clopas
Mary Magdalene
Mother & Beloved Disciple
"Behold: your son."
"Behold: your mother."

CROSS

63

SOME OBSERVATIONS

The crucifixion is told in the briefest and starkest terms possible, without dwelling on the physical details of Jesus' suffering (though these are certainly part of the passage).

Daniel J. Harrington, S.J. (NJBC)

In John, the mockeries of a crown of thorns and a purple robe happen <u>before</u> Pilate tries to shame the crowds into letting Jesus go free, saying *Behold the Man!* In Matthew and Mark, this mockery happens <u>after</u> Pilate delivers him to be crucified. In Luke, the mockery with *gorgeous apparel* happens at the hands of Herod's soldiers. Did this shared mockery make Herod and Pilate friends?

If scarlet red in Matthew was the color worn by soldiers, it would be more handy than the probably more expensive "royal" color of purple mentioned in Mark.

Since Simon of Cyrene is named in Mark as the father of Alexander and Rufus, these two sons of the Cyrenian were likely known to the community for whom Mark was originally written. Simon takes up the cross against his will. At some level, don't we all? In Luke, faithful to the theme of being called to *follow* Jesus, Simon carries the cross *behind Jesus.*

John makes no mention of Simon of Cyrene; perhaps his community did not have this tradition. In carrying his own cross, is Jesus saying he is *still in control?*

Luke tells us there is a large crowd, a great multitude, adding to the intensity of Jesus' circumstance, and helping us to imagine the many witnesses there.

Only Luke reports Jesus' consoling words to the Daughters of Jerusalem: *Do not weep for me, but weep for yourselves and for your children*. Does it seem strange that at this point in the story Jesus would have enough energy to minister to the lamenting women?

Mountains, fall on us; hills, cover us. These words are from the prophesy of Hosea, that Israel's luxury and abundance will be lost (Hosea 10:8b). The saying about green wood (with sap) contrasts it with dry wood ready to burn. The *Revised Standard Version* footnote suggests:

> *If an innocent man is thus punished,*
> *what must the guilty (dry wood) expect?*

Golgotha is a small stone hill just outside the city walls, near an abandoned quarry. The Greek name *Golgotha* is a transliteration, like a phonetic spelling of the Aramaic word *gulgulta'*, meaning *skull*. The word *skull* refers either to the shape or the use of the place. In the days of Jesus, it was outside the walls of Jerusalem. In today's Jerusalem, this place is marked by the Church of the Holy Sepulchre, now within a part of the city that has been walled-in. The name *Calvary* is from the Latin word for skull, *calvaria*.

The garments of the crucified are plunder for the executing soldiers, who were likely recruited by the Romans from Palestine or Syria. Psalm 22:19 is one reference for dividing up and gambling over the garments. When a person lost his or her liberty, he or she also lost the ability to wear clothes. Old Testament examples include:

CROSS

> *prisoners and slaves* (See Deut. 28:48; Isaiah 20:2-4),
> *prostitutes* (Ez 16:38-40), *demented people* (1 Sam 19:23-24),
> *and the damned* (1 Samuel 28:14).

Free identity can be signified by clothing. So when Harry Potter gives clothing (a sock) to Dobby the House Elf, he sets him free. Art notwithstanding, there is no biblical suggestion that any covering would have been allowed to one being crucified. Will this make more prominent the witness of the Centurion who will publicly admit that he is *Son of God?* (We haven't gotten there in the story yet.)

> *A slave's death on the cross is not poetry*
> *but bitter historical reality.*
>
> Benedict T. Viviano, O.P. (NJBC)

The death of Jesus on a cross would have been such a scandal, creating such difficulties to those who spread the story of Jesus, that the scandalous nature of the cross is one of the historical indicators that it happened this way.

The circle of those who are reviling Jesus closes in, from the passersby (representing the crowds), to the priests and scribes, and finally by the robbers crucified with him.

Luke tells us of the repentant thief, the good criminal. Like the story of the prodigal son, this can be called a *gospel within the Gospel...*

> *The criminal has deep faith that the dying Jesus*
> *is truly a king and can dispense the pardon*
> *and mercy which only a king can.*
>
> Robert J. Karris, O.F.M.(NJBC)

Jesus gives him the greatest pardon: freedom from sin.

THE PASSION IN THE GREAT STORY OF JESUS

The paradise promise is timed: today, this day, no need to wait. The rich image of paradise is the garden given Adam and Eve with the fruit of the tree of life. Its gates were closed by human sin but are are this day *reopened* by the *New Adam*.

The titles on the inscription vary a bit, but they all say *King of the Jews* (literally *King of the Judeans*). The priests have a problem with this, but Pilate will not change it. John emphasizes *the public and universal character of the inscription, since it could be read by all: Jews, Greeks, and Romans.*

Only in the gospel of John is Mary the mother of Jesus at the scene, not *afar*, but there at the cross. Pheme Perkins pondered *the relationship between this tradition* (in John) *that Mary comes under the care of the Beloved Disciple and that in Acts 1:14 which* (later) *places her and the brothers of Jesus in the circle gathered around the Twelve,* and how *entrusting the Beloved Disciple and his mother to each other shows that Jesus' mission is completed in the care and provision that Jesus has made for 'his own.'* How much of his suffering is their shared admission that Mary cannot halt his pain?

Megan McKenna observes that as Mary is mother to us all *devotion to her is dangerous to any existing form of power or structure of individuals that treat other human beings as worthless, expendable or as an enemy. She appears in history to remind Christians that those who call themselves her children must be brothers and sisters to all her children.* Being brothers and sisters of one mother makes us dangerous to power structures that seek to keep us divided. The varied stories of appearances of Mary are in just such circumstances.

CROSS

The care Jesus shows from the cross for the good criminal, the beloved disciple, and Mary are profound reminders of God's care for us that never ends.

In Luke, Jesus asks the Father to *forgive them, for they know not what they do.* Who are *"them"*? For whom is Jesus asking forgiveness? There are many people in Luke who knew not what they did:

→ the chief priests, who came with each other
and brought their servants too (The bad thing
can be easier to do when it is done in a crowd.),

→ the chiefs of the temple guards, who made sure
that this troublemaker who threatened their jobs
was dealt with aright,

→ the *ancients,* who helped to arrest him, presbyters,
elders who have gained respect,

→ the high priest, who thinks he is doing the
right thing, protecting things as they are,

→ the apostles, who ate and drank with him,
and then kept their distance,

→ Judas, who betrayed him,

→ Peter, who denied him,

→ the servant girl by the fire, who innocently
tried to get Peter on the hook,

→ the guards, who mocked and slapped the Lord,

→ the council of elders (presbyters), chief priests,
and scribes, who met early and in secret,

→ Pilate, who saw no case against Jesus,
and who could not accept the grace
to see who really stood before him,

68 — THE PASSION IN THE GREAT STORY OF JESUS

➜ Herod, who for a long time had wanted
to see this man, but who could also not see
the true Son of God,

➜ Barabbas, who took his awkward freedom
and ran,

➜ Simon of Cyrene, who carried the cross
and then gave it back,

➜ The daughters of Jerusalem, who could do
no more than weep,

➜ the Beloved Disciple, who fell asleep
while Jesus was in agony,

Forgiveness is hard because it involves loving other people in spite of the evil that they have done to us. When we forgive, we don't deny the hurt that we have received. We don't deny that it was wrong. We don't pretend that nothing happened. But we acknowledge that there is more to the offender than the offense. It is that 'more' that we (come to) see when we forgive; it is that 'more that we love in spite of the offense.'

Bishop Daniel Pilarczyk

OK, so Jesus was and is the Son of God. Was forgiveness easier for him? In Luke, Jesus says *and if he sins against you seven times in the day, and turns to you seven times, and says, 'I repent,' you must forgive him* (Luke 17:4). And in Matthew, it was Peter whom Jesus tells to forgive his brother 70 times 7 times, translated by some to mean 77 times. 70 times 7 equals 490 times. *From-the-cross* was clearly not the first time that Jesus asked the Father to forgive. Clearly, forgiveness is part of the *being* of Jesus.

CROSS

Martin Luther King, Jr. wrote that a human being

> *cannot forgive up to four hundred and ninety times*
> *without forgiveness becoming a part*
> *of the 'habit structure of his being.'*
> *Forgiveness is not an occasional act;*
> *it is a permanent attitude.* Martin Luther King, Jr.

This may be cheating, an easy way out; but if we are finding forgiveness impossible, perhaps Jesus is giving us an out that is really an entrance, a way to begin. If I cannot yet say the words, *I forgive you* or *I pardon you*, can I pray for all who are still unhealed, with the words of Jesus on the Cross and say as he said, *Father, forgive them, for they know not what they do.* And Father, forgive us when we do.

ADDITIONAL QUESTIONS

1. Did I notice anything else in the scripture text?

2. Who does today's world like to crucify?
   Why?

3. Have I accepted the grace to name my cross?
   How am I doing with picking it up daily?

4. Who might God be calling me to forgive?
   What if there is danger of me being hurt again?

THE PASSION IN THE GREAT STORY OF JESUS

CLOSING PRAYER

Are there intercessions from the group?

then continue with the
STATIONS OF THE CROSS
Arranged by Pope John Paul II, 1991
Group members take turns leading.

1st Jesus is in agony in the Garden of Olives
(pause 10 seconds)

LEADER   *We adore you, O Christ, and we bless you.*

ALL   **Because by your holy cross
you have redeemed the world.**

2nd Jesus is betrayed by Judas and arrested.
(pause 10 seconds)

LEADER   *We adore you...*   *ALL*   **Because by...**

3rd Jesus is condemned by the Sanhedrin.
(pause 10 seconds)

LEADER   *We adore you...*   *ALL*   **Because by...**

4th Jesus is denied by Peter.
(pause 10 seconds)

LEADER   *We adore you...*   *ALL*   **Because by...**

5th Jesus is condemned by Pilate.
(pause 10 seconds)

LEADER   *We adore you...*   *ALL*   **Because by...**

6th Jesus is scourged and crowned with thorns.
(pause 10 seconds)

LEADER   *We adore you...*   *ALL*   **Because by...**

CROSS

7th **Jesus is made to carry his cross.**
(pause 10 seconds)
LEADER *We adore you...*   *ALL* **Because by...**

8th **Simon of Cyrene helps Jesus carry his cross.**
(pause 10 seconds)
LEADER *We adore you...*   *ALL* **Because by...**

9th **Jesus meets the women of Jerusalem.**
(pause 10 seconds)
LEADER *We adore you...*   *ALL* **Because by...**

10th **Jesus is crucified.**
(pause 10 seconds)
LEADER *We adore you...*   *ALL* **Because by...**

11th **Jesus promises the Kingdom
to the repentant thief.**
(pause 10 seconds)
LEADER *We adore you...*   *ALL* **Because by...**

12th **Jesus speaks to his mother
and to the beloved disciple.**
(pause 10 seconds)
LEADER *We adore you...*   *ALL* **Because by...**

13th **Jesus dies on the cross.**
(pause 10 seconds)
LEADER *We adore you...*   *ALL* **Because by...**

14th **Jesus is laid in the tomb.**
(pause 10 seconds)
LEADER *We adore you...*   *ALL* **Because by...**

Continue with Psalm 22 on pages 20-21.

View of the North End of Jerusalem, Looking East (30 A.D.)

To catch your bearings, see the map on page 22.

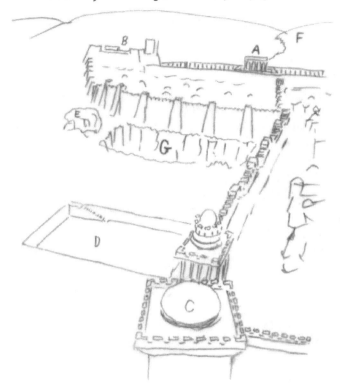

Adapted from a drawing from Fr. Raymond E. Brown, S.S.,
The Passion Narratives of the Gospels, **a course on tape**

A. The Temple (Second Temple, built 520-515 B.C.,
     refurbished by Herod the Great, beginning 20-19 B.C.)
B. Fortress Antonia, a Hasmonean castle refurbished by Herod about 35 B.C.
C. The Herodian Palace on the West Hill, built by Herod about 23 B.C.
D. Hezekiah's Pool which stood outside the city in Jesus' time
E. Golgotha (Calvary, Skull Hill) where Jesus was crucified, near which he was buried (now the site of the Church of the Holy Sepulchre)
F. Mount of Olives in the distance, East of the city across the Kidron Valley
G. A quarried out area at the base of the walls

Week 5
death

Opening Prayer: Keep a finger here and join in
the Song on the back cover.

Someone reads the Faith Sharing Ground Rules, page 5.

> Members of the group read: **Matthew 27:45-56** *from their personal bibles*,
> one verse at a time, taking turns.
> When it is your turn to read a verse,
> take a silent breath before reading it.
> As each verse is being read aloud,
> other members read along silently . . .

Before going further, let each member of the group name *one* word, phrase, or image that caught his or her attention. Do this *without* any comment or explanation. There is time for that later . . .

Then, take five minutes to review the Passion Narrative Comparative Text on the next five pages, in silence.

THE PASSION IN THE GREAT STORY OF JESUS

THE DEATH OF JESUS (the text)

Matthew 27:45-50

45 Now
from the <u>sixth hour</u>
<u>darkness</u> comes over all the land
<u>until the ninth hour</u>.

46 And about the ninth hour,
Jesus cries out with a <u>loud voice</u>,
saying,
"<u>Eli, Eli, lema sabachthani?</u>"
This is,
"<u>My God, my God,</u>
 <u>why have you forsaken me?</u>"

47 And some of the ones
standing there hearing say,
"<u>This man calls Elijah</u>."
48 And immediately one of them
running and taking a <u>sponge</u>
and filling with <u>vinegar</u>
and placing it <u>around a reed</u>
gives him <u>to drink</u>.
49 But the rest say,
"Let him be; let us see
 if Elijah comes to save him."
50 And Jesus again cries out
with a <u>loud voice</u>

and <u>releases his spirit</u>.

Mark 15:33-37

33 And becoming
the <u>sixth hour</u> *(noon)*
<u>darkness</u> comes over all the land
<u>until the ninth hour</u> *(3 p.m.)*.

34 And at the ninth hour
Jesus cries with a <u>loud voice</u>,

"<u>Eloi, Eloi, lama sabachthani?</u>"
which means,
"<u>My God, my God,</u>
 <u>why have you forsaken me?</u>"

35 And some of the ones
standing by hearing say,
"Behold: <u>he calls Elijah</u>."
36 And one
running having <u>filled a sponge</u>
<u>with vinegar</u>
placing it <u>around a reed</u>
gives him <u>to drink</u>,
saying,
"Let him be; let us see
 if Elijah comes to take him down."
37 But Jesus lets go
a <u>loud voice</u>

and <u>breathes his last</u>.

DEATH   75

THE DEATH OF JESUS (the text)

Luke 23:44-46   ## John 19:28-30

44 And it is now about   28 After this, knowing
the <u>sixth hour</u>   that all things are now finished,
and <u>darkness</u> comes over all the land   that the scripture might be fulfilled,
<u>until the ninth hour</u>.

45 As the <u>sun fails</u>,
the <u>veil of the temple</u> is <u>torn</u>.

                                     Jesus says,
                                     "<u>I thirst</u>."

                                     29 A <u>jar full of vinegar</u> sits there,
                                     and so a <u>sponge</u> full of the <u>vinegar</u>
                                     put round a <u>hyssop</u>,
                                     they bring it <u>to his mouth</u>.
                                     30 And so when Jesus has
                                     taken the vinegar, he says,
                                     "<u>It is finished</u>."

46 And voicing out
with a <u>loud voice</u>
Jesus says,
"<u>Father, into your hands</u>
 <u>I commend my spirit</u>."
And saying this   And bowing his head
he <u>breathes his last</u>.   he <u>gives up his spirit</u>.

THE PASSION IN THE GREAT STORY OF JESUS

WITNESSING THE DEATH (the text)

Matthew 27:51-56

51 And behold:
the <u>veil of the temple</u> is <u>rent in two</u>
from <u>top to bottom</u>,
and the <u>earth quakes</u>
and the <u>rocks are split</u>,
52 and the <u>tombs are opened</u>
and <u>bodies of many holy ones</u>
who had fallen asleep <u>are raised</u>,
53 and coming forth out of
the tombs enter the holy city
and <u>appear after his rising to many</u>.
54 And the <u>centurion</u> and the
ones guarding Jesus with him,
seeing the earthquake and
the things happening
fear exceedingly, saying,
"<u>Truly this man was the Son of God</u>."

55 Now there are <u>many women</u>
there <u>beholding from afar</u>,
who followed Jesus from Galilee
and <u>ministered</u> to him.
56 Among them are
<u>Mary the Magdalene</u>, and <u>Mary</u>
<u>the mother of James and of Joseph</u>,
and the <u>mother of the sons</u>
<u>of Zebedee</u>.

Mark 15:38-41

38 And
the <u>veil of the temple</u> is <u>rent in two</u>
from <u>top to bottom</u>.

39 And the <u>centurion</u> standing by
opposite him
seeing
how he breathed his last,
says,
"<u>Truly this man was the Son of God</u>."

40 Now there are also <u>women</u>
<u>beholding from afar</u>,

including both
<u>Mary the Magdalene</u> and <u>Mary</u>
<u>the mother of James the younger and</u>
<u>Joses</u>, and <u>Salome</u>,

41 who <u>followed him</u>
when he was in Galilee
and <u>ministered to him</u>,
and <u>many others</u> who
had come up with him to Jerusalem.

DEATH

WITNESSING THE DEATH (the text)

Luke 23:47-49

John 19:31-37

31 And so since it is <u>Preparation Day</u>,
that the bodies might not remain
on the cross on the Sabbath,
for <u>great is the day of this Sabbath</u>,
the Judeans ask Pilate that
their legs might be broken
and they might be taken.
32 And so the <u>soldiers</u> come
and <u>break the legs of the first</u>
<u>and of the other</u> crucified with him.
33 But <u>coming on Jesus</u>,

47 And seeing the thing happening
the <u>centurion</u>

when <u>they see him already dead</u>,
<u>they do not break his legs</u>,
34 but one of the soldiers
<u>pierces his side with a lance</u>,
and immediately

<u>glorifies God</u> saying,
"<u>For sure this was a just man</u>."

<u>blood and water come out</u>.

48 And all the <u>crowds</u> arrive
and see and behold
the things happening,
and <u>return beating their breasts</u>.
49 And all <u>the ones known to him</u>
<u>stand far off</u>, and <u>the women</u>
accompanying him from Galilee,
<u>see these things</u>.

35 And the one who saw this
has witnessed, and his witness is true,
and that one knows
that <u>he speaks truly</u>,
<u>that you may believe</u>.
36 For these things have happened
that the scripture might be fulfilled,
  Not a bone of his shall be broken.

37 And again another scripture says,
  They shall look at him
  whom they pierced.

THE PASSION IN THE GREAT STORY OF JESUS

MATTHEW 27:45-56

Sixth hour darkness
Ninth hour: *"My God,
    my God, why have you
    abandoned me?"*
Vinegar is offered
J's loud voice

J releases his spirit
Curtain is torn
Earthquake
Dead are raised & walk
Centurion: *Son of God*
4 women see from afar

MARK 15:33-41

Sixth hour darkness
Ninth hour: *"My God,
    my God, why have you
    abandoned me?"*
Vinegar is offered
J's loud voice

J breathes his last
Curtain is torn

Centurion: *Son of God*
4 women see from afar

LUKE 23:44-49

Sixth hour darkness
Eclipse; curtain is torn

J's loud voice
"I commend my spirit"
J breathes his last

Centurion: *Innocent*
Bystanders repent
Women see

JOHN 19:28-37

"I thirst"
Vinegar is offered

"It is finished"
J gives up his spirit
Jews want bodies
    removed
Soldiers break legs
Pierce J's side

DEATH

79

SOME OBSERVATIONS

Mahatma Gandhi called the crucifixion *the perfect act of nonviolence*. As we say that Jesus' complete offering of himself was out of complete love for us, can we call it *the perfect act of love?*

The darkness from the sixth hour (noon) *to the ninth hour* (3 pm) *has been variously interpreted as a sandstorm, an eclipse of the sun, or the fulfillment of Amos 8:9.*   Harrington

Jesus' cry, *Eloi, Eloi* (Mark) or *Eli, Eli* (Matthew) is an Aramaic version of the beginning words of Psalm 22: *My God, my God, why have you forsaken me.* It is a psalm of lament, a prayer of an innocent person, one who is suffering and feels very much abandoned, left alone, a cry to God. To pray Psalm 22 is to enter into the center of abandonment, but not of despair; lonely, given up on, withdrawn from, deserted, left entirely, but crying out, even loudly, to our God.

Psalm 22 admits distress in graphic image, **and** the singer remembers God's mercy. Jesus: beaten, stripped, mocked, dying a death of the God-forsaken, sings loudly the beginning of this psalm of his people. *Jesus-on-the-cross* helps us to face squarely whether our troubles are like those of a spoiled child (*Nobody likes me, everybody hates me, might as well go eat worms*) or like those of a child of God at the center of the mystery of what it sometimes is to be a Christian:

➔   wracked by deep human suffering,
➔   aware, at the core, of being loved by God,
➔   and carrying them both on mission,
     calling others into that love.

Psalm 22 could be seen, then, as an example of what Saint Ignatius of Loyola called "hard consolation:" being in deep pain but consoled in one's inmost being by God's abiding loving presence.

In Luke, the vinegar is a prop for mocking Jesus, but in the other gospels it is not so clear. It could have been intended to help ease Jesus' pain, especially after his words: *I thirst.* It does fulfill the prophesy, *for my thirst they gave me vinegar* (Psalm 69:22b). A reed had been used as a scepter to mock him; is it now used with a sponge of vinegar as an instrument of compassion? Or does the mocking continue? Sometimes it is hard to tell the difference. Psalm 69 suggests that the offer of sour wine is a hostile gesture.

In John his final words are <u>spoken</u>, *It is finished,* in contrast to the loud voice in Luke <u>crying out</u> to the Father, *Into your hands I commend my spirit* (Psalm 31:6). Both suggest that Jesus' life was not *taken* by anyone, but given *willingly* by him.

In Mark and Matthew, *a sudden violent death* is specified without details, breathing his last (Mark) and releasing his spirit (Matthew). Matthew leans more to a death that was voluntary, a freely given gift.

In the desert wanderings, Moses wore a veil after his encounters with God because the shine on his face was so bright that people could not look at him. The temple curtain torn top to bottom speaks of a new age in salvation history. The torn temple is already being rebuilt. Though the veil reverently separated the people from God, in the Son's ministry God touched his people.

DEATH

81

In John, the death of Jesus is certified by the soldiers before he is buried. They pierce his side with a lance, and *blood and water* flow out. In Maccabees, there is a story of blood and water flowing out of the side of one of the martyrs (4 Macc 9:20). It is said that as the lambs were sacrificed in the temple, the blood of the lambs would mingle with the springs of water flowing out of Jerusalem. Blood and water may simply be a reference to the sacraments of Eucharist and Baptism.

Jesus would have lost a great deal of blood from the scourging and be dehydrated, in a weak condition. But the cause of death in a crucifixion was usually suffocation. The crucified man, weakened, would keep pulling himself up to expand his chest cavity and take in a breath. This would go on and on, until he no longer had the strength to do so, and he would suffocate.

In the second creation account in Genesis 1, God formed the man, *'adam*, out of clay, and then breathed into his nostrils the breath of life. God continues to be present to us, now with the Son, through the Holy Spirit. Spirit means *wind, breath, air moving*. As long as we are taking in the breath of life, God is still growing and shaping us into the men and women God created us to be. And we strangled his Son.

Bones of a man crucified in this time show that the legs may have been broken to hasten the suffocation if a quicker death was desired. Pheme Perkins adds that: *If the passage intended to parallel Jesus with the Passover lamb, then the rule against breaking the lamb's bones would be its origin* (Exodus 12:10; Numbers 9:12).

In Luke, when the assembled crowd saw what happened, they went home, beating their breasts, a sign of repentance. Even after doing this to the one now proclaimed *innocent* or *just* by the pagan centurion, reconciliation with God is still possible. Is there irony in how this paschal gift is the crux of our redemption?

Still at the cross stand the women. The Twelve are only there in Luke, and only from afar.

If we did not know this person, Jesus of Nazareth, we might be able to hear the story and watch his dying as simple bystanders, faces in the crowd. What if this was happening to your best friend? Would you be able to stay there and watch without saying or doing anything? Would you be able to simply walk away? Would you be able to revisit the gruesome story every year?

On Good Friday, we are disciples, followers, students, and servants at the feet of our master. Jesus claims us as companions, co-heirs, friends. Right before telling us in John's gospel to love one another, Jesus proclaims, *I have called you friends* (John 15:15).

A few years ago a good friend tried to describe to me his own friendship with Jesus. You know how it is. You do different things together, stretched over time, including celebrations, real crises, even dull routines, massive amounts of time spent and even wasted together. One day, suddenly you become aware and realize with gratitude, *Hey, this is my friend!* Even if you don't say what you just realized, you know that when this person suffers again, so will you.

DEATH

The pain of the Cross is so acute that there is only one way that we can bear to hear this story about this friend. Wherever we are in the deepening of that intimacy, in the celebrations, routines and crises of life with Christ, the only way we can bear to hear this story is with some awareness already of the Risen Lord, risen in our midst, with the Father and still to come.

Already aware that Christ rose from this death, we can remember and somehow taste and join in the shock and fear and sadness of the original disciples.

Lifted up on the cross, lifted up in our midst, lifted up with the Father, as Jesus had said, *When I am lifted up from the earth, I will draw everyone to myself* (John 12:32). With the power of those words of Jesus, we can let what our tradition calls *the seven last words of Jesus* ring in our ears:

1. *Father, forgive them...*

2. *This day in paradise...*

3. *See your son; see your mother...*

4. *My God, my God why have you forsaken me?*

5. *I am thirsty...*

6. *It is finished...*

7. *I commend my spirit...*

84 THE PASSION IN THE GREAT STORY OF JESUS

ADDITIONAL QUESTIONS

1. Did I notice anything else in the scripture text?

2. Cardinal Joseph Bernardin of Chicago,
   in his book *The Gift of Peace,* wrote of
   the grace of coming to see death as his friend.
   How is such a thing possible?

3. Is there anything I fear more than dying?

4. When have I felt abandoned or forsaken?
   How might God have been there?

5. Why do we pray for the dead and the dying?

CLOSING PRAYER

Are there intercessions from the group?

then continue with the
GOOD FRIDAY REPROACHES
(Adapted from the Roman Missal)
Group members take turns leading.

1. *I led you from slavery to freedom,
     and you handed me over to the chief priests.*
     ALL **My people, how have I grieved you?**

2. *I opened before you the sea,
     and you opened my side with a lance.*
     ALL **My people, how have I grieved you?**

DEATH

3. *I led you in a pillar of cloud,*
   and you led me into Pilate's palace.

   ALL **My people, how have I grieved you?**

4. *I fed you with manna in the desert,*
   and you rained on me blows and lashes.

   ALL **My people, how have I grieved you?**

5. *I gave you saving water from the rock to drink,*
   and you gave me gall and vinegar.

   ALL **My people, how have I grieved you?**

6. *I struck down for you the kings of Canaan,*
   and you struck my head with a reed.

   ALL **My people, how have I grieved you?**

7. *I put in your hand a royal scepter,*
   and you put on my head a crown of thorns.

   ALL **My people, how have I grieved you?**

8. *I raised you to great power,*
   and you raised me up on the cross.

   ALL **My people, how have I grieved you?**

Continue with a portion of Psalm 31:

ALL **Into your hands I commend my spirit;**
You redeem me, Lord God of truth...

Be strong and strengthen your heart,
All you hoping in the Lord.

SONG OF THE SUFFERING SERVANT
Isaiah 52:13 - 53:5

SIDE 1   See, my servant will act wisely,
and be raised and lifted up and exalted highly!

SIDE 2   *Just as many were appalled at him,*
so disfigured beyond human appearance,
and his form beyond that of human sons,

SIDE 1   So will he sprinkle many nations;
because of him kings will shut their mouth.

SIDE 2   *For what was not told to them they will see*
and what they did not hear they will understand.

SIDE 1   Who has believed what we have heard?
To whom has the arm of the Lord been revealed?

SIDE 2   *Now he grew up like a sapling before him,*
and like the root out of dry ground;

SIDE 1   No beauty is to him, nor majesty that attracts us,
nor appearance that would make us desire him.

SIDE 2   *He was despised and rejected by human beings,*
a man of sorrows, one familiar with suffering,

SIDE 1   like one around whom people hide their faces,
he was despised, and we did not esteem him.

SIDE 2   *Surely he took up our infirmities*
and carried our sorrows.

SIDE 1   Yet we considered him as one being stricken,
as one smitten by God and afflicted.

SIDE 2   *But he is pierced for our transgressions*
and crushed for our iniquities.

SIDE 1   Upon him is the punishment that brings us peace;
by his wounds is his healing upon us.

Week 6
burial

Opening Prayer: Keep a finger here and join in the Song on the back cover.

← then, *Song of the Suffering Servant*

Someone reads the Faith Sharing Ground Rules, page 5.

Members of the group read: **Mark 15:42-47** *from their personal bibles,* one verse at a time, taking turns. When it is your turn to read a verse, take a silent breath before reading it. As each verse is being read aloud, other members read along silently . . .

Before going further, let each member of the group name *one* word, phrase, or image that caught his or her attention. Do this *without* any comment or explanation. There is time for that later . . .

☦

Then, take five minutes to review the Passion Narrative Comparative Text on the next three pages, in silence.

THE PASSION IN THE GREAT STORY OF JESUS

THE BURIAL (the text)

Matthew 27:57-61

57 Now <u>evening</u> has come;

a <u>rich man from Arimathea</u>,
named <u>Joseph</u>

who is also himself
<u>discipled to Jesus</u>,

58 <u>approaching Pilate</u>
<u>asks for the body</u> of Jesus.

Then <u>Pilate commands</u>
it be given to him.
59 And <u>taking the body</u>
<u>Joseph wraps</u> it
in a <u>piece of unused linen</u>

and <u>lays it in his new tomb</u>
which he had <u>hewn in the rock</u>,
and <u>rolling a great stone</u>
to the door of the tomb,
<u>goes away</u>.

61 And there <u>Mary Magdalene</u>
and <u>the other Mary</u>
<u>sit opposite the grave</u>.

Mark 15:42-47

42 And now with evening coming
since it is the <u>Preparation Day</u>,
<u>the day before the Sabbath</u>,
43 <u>Joseph from Arimathea</u>,
a <u>distinguished member of the council</u>,

who is also himself
<u>expecting the kingdom of God</u>,

taking courage comes and goes <u>to Pilate</u>
and <u>asks for the body</u> of Jesus. 44 And
Pilate is <u>astonished as to whether</u>
<u>he has already died</u>, and calling to him
the <u>centurion</u> questions him how long
since he had died.

45 And knowing from the centurion
he <u>grants the body to Joseph</u>.
46 And <u>having bought</u>
<u>a piece of unused linen</u>, taking
<u>him down</u> he <u>wraps</u> with the linen

and <u>lays him in a tomb</u>
which had been <u>hewn out of rock</u>,
and <u>rolls a stone</u>
against the door of the tomb.

47 And <u>Mary the Magdalene</u>
and <u>Mary the mother of Joses</u>
<u>see where he is laid</u>.

16:1 And when the Sabbath has passed,
Mary the Magdalene, and Mary the
mother of James, and Salome buy spices
that they might come and anoint him.

BURIAL

89

THE BURIAL (the text)

Luke 23:50-56

John 19:38-42

50 And behold:

38 Now after these things

a man named <u>Joseph</u>,
a <u>member of the council</u>,
<u>a good and just man</u>, <u>not agreeing</u>
<u>with the council</u> and their action,
from a <u>Judean town of Arimathea</u>,
who was <u>awaiting the kingdom of God</u>,

<u>Joseph from Arimathea</u>,

<u>a disciple of Jesus</u> though <u>in secret</u>
because of <u>fear of the Judeans</u>,

52 this man <u>approaching Pilate</u>
<u>asks for the body</u> of Jesus,

<u>asks Pilate</u>
<u>that he might take the body</u> of Jesus;

and <u>Pilate allows it</u>.
And so he comes and takes his body.
39 And <u>also Nicodemus</u>, <u>who had</u>
<u>first come to him by night</u>, comes
bearing a mixture of <u>myrrh and aloes</u>,
<u>about a hundred litras</u> (*about 75 pounds*).

53 and <u>taking down</u>
<u>wraps it in linen</u>

40 And so they <u>take the body</u> of Jesus
and <u>bind it in linens with the spices</u>,
as is the burial custom of the Judeans.
41 Now there is <u>in the place where</u>
<u>he has been crucified</u> <u>a garden</u>,

and <u>lays him in a rock-hewn tomb</u>
<u>where no one had yet been laid</u>.
54 And it is <u>Preparation Day</u>
and <u>a Sabbath is coming</u>.
55 And the <u>women</u> following,
having come <u>out of Galilee</u>
with him, <u>behold the tomb</u>
and <u>how the body is laid</u>,
56 and returning
prepare <u>spices and ointment</u>.
And <u>on the Sabbath</u>,
<u>indeed they rest</u>
according to the commandment.

and in the garden <u>a new tomb</u>,
<u>in which no one has ever been laid</u>.
42 And so because of the
<u>Preparation Day of the Judeans</u>,
<u>since the tomb is near</u>,
<u>there they lay Jesus</u>.

THE PASSION IN THE GREAT STORY OF JESUS

GUARD AT THE TOMB (the text)

Matthew 27:62-66

62 And the <u>next day</u>, <u>after the Day of Preparation</u>,
The <u>chief priests and the Pharisees</u> assemble <u>to Pilate</u>, 63 saying,
"Lord, we remember what that imposter said while still living,
'After three days I am raised.'
64 and so, <u>command that the grave be kept secure until the third day</u>,
lest the disciples may steal him and say to the people he was raised from
the dead, the last imposture being worse than the first."
65 Pilate says to them,
"<u>You have a guard</u>; <u>you go and make it secure as you know</u>."
66 And going <u>with the guard</u>, they secure the grave, <u>sealing the stone</u>."

MATTHEW 27:57-66
Joseph of Arimathea

Body is wrapped
    in unused linen
New rock tomb
Stone against the door
Mary Magdalene &
    other Mary
Guard

MARK 15:42-47
Joseph of Arimathea
Pilate checks on the death
Body is wrapped
    in unused linen
Rock tomb
Stone against the door
Mary Magdalene &
    Mary (Joses' mother)

LUKE 23:50-56
Joseph of Arimathea

Body is wrapped
    in linen
Unused rock tomb
Preparation Day
Women from Galilee
They prepare spices

JOHN 19:38-42
Joseph of Arimathea
Nicodemus
Spices and ointment
Body in linens & spices
Unused garden tomb
Preparation Day

BURIAL

91

SOME OBSERVATIONS

1st Corinthians, chapter 15, may give us the oldest baptismal creed we have, perhaps the one in which Saint Paul was baptized in Damascus:

> *For I handed on to you, among the first things,*
> *what I also received,*
> *that, Christ died on behalf of our sins,*
> > *according to the scriptures,*
> *and that, he was buried,*
> *and that, he was raised on the third day,*
> > *according to the scriptures,*
> *and that, he was seen by Cephas, then by the Twelve;*
> > *...seen by over five hundred...by James...*
> > *...by all the Apostles...also by me* (Paul).
>
> 1st Corinthians 15:3-8

As the appearances and the "sightings," can serve as a kind of "proof" of the resurrection, so can the burial be seen as a kind of "proof" of his death. Though we rely on faith and not on proof, this detail can be helpful when dealing with "gnostics" or others who would deny the humanity of Jesus and suggest that Jesus was fully God but only appeared to be human. Our belief is in the two natures of Jesus: fully God **and** fully human. Efforts through the centuries to lift up either of his two natures to the detriment of the other has a name: *heresy*.

> *Just as Jesus shared with us*
> *the experience of a mother's womb,*
> *so he shares with humanity*
> *the experience of a grave.*

The burial is the necessary preparation for the story of the empty tomb. Mary Magdalene is the connecting witness; she saw Jesus die, knew where he was buried, and went to the tomb on Easter. The Sabbath would begin at sunset on Friday afternoon, and the burial needed to happen before the day of rest began, or it would have to wait until the Sabbath was over. Mark does not specify that Joseph of Arimathea was a follower of Jesus, and assumes that he was part of the Sanhedrin that condemned Jesus. He found his courage.

Does Pilate's doubt in Mark about the death of Jesus spring from his encounter with him? It's unlikely. He sends soldiers who know what death looks like.

In Matthew, Joseph of Arimathea is no longer said to be a member of the Sanhedrin, which was after all responsible for the death of Jesus, but is rather *a disciple of Jesus*. Matthew has Jesus buried in a tomb intended for a rich man.

As Luke suggests, if Joseph of Arimathea was a member of the Sanhedrin, then the decision of the religious leaders against Jesus was not unanimous.

The secrecy of Joseph's discipleship and that of Nicodemus is maintained in the pious act of burying the dead. This could be how Nicodemus entered the tradition of the gospel of John, revealing later the night visit.

Matthew omits Mark's questions of Pilate to the centurion, but will use the soldiers in another way in the resurrection accounts.

Perhaps this is a question only a retired accountant might ask: When in Mark did Joseph buy the linen?

BURIAL

In Matthew the greatness of the stone is left out. According to some excavations in the area, the tomb may have been a quarry no longer used rather than in a cemetery for the rich and famous. This is consistent with Mark's more simple description.

Archeology around Jerusalem has revealed tombs from the first century of dug-out limestone caves with one or more shelves on which to lay the body or bodies, with a large circular stone to close the opening. After a year of decay, the bones would be retrieved and put in a stone box called an ossuary, perhaps with bones of other family members. This suggests that a tomb might normally be used more than once.

Robert Karris points to linen as a symbol of immortality, made from the fiber of flax growing from the earth. In Luke, having openly disagreed with the council and with hope in the resurrection, Joseph wraps the body with linen. This detail also reminds us of the infant Jesus being wrapped in swaddling clothes. Peter will find these cloths alone.

John's 75 pounds of myrrh and aloes show the great honor Joseph and Nicodemus intended to give to the body of this great King. This is no common grave. Compared to Mark's single linen, John describes an anointing and binding likely in strips of linen, as had been done for Lazarus (John 11:43-44).

Movie accounts of the raising of Lazarus make a great show of a strong stench coming from the tomb. Perhaps this memory is on their mind as they are perhaps a bit excessive with the spices for the body.

Again, John tells us that both the crucifixion and the burial are in a garden, where Mary Magdalene and the others will go on Easter morning. The women are witnesses to the burial in Matthew and Mark and Luke. Since the testimony of women did not carry much weight in their law, this is one of those details seen by scholars as giving the account greater credence.

What happened while he was in the tomb? This we will find out in heaven. Our tradition tells us in the Nicene Creed (from the Council of Nicea, 325 A.D.) simply that *he suffered death and was buried.* The Apostles' Creed adds that *he descended into hell,* or as in the old Sacramentary, *he descended to the dead.* Rather than implying that Jesus had to go to hell, this tradition is that in his passion and death, Jesus goes to the very limits of Godforsakenness. No one who has ever felt forsaken by God is beyond the reach of the Crucified/Risen Christ.

Listen to what the Catechism adds about the burial of Jesus, rooted in the Nicene and Apostles' Creeds:

> *In his plan of salvation, God ordained that his Son should not only 'die for our sins' but also 'taste death,' experience the condition of death, the separation of his soul from his body, between the time he expired on the cross and the time he was raised from the dead. The state of the dead Christ is the mystery of the tomb and the descent into hell. It is the mystery of Holy Saturday, when Christ, lying in the tomb, reveals God's great*

BURIAL

Sabbath rest after the fulfillment of the salvation of humanity, which brings peace to the whole universe.

(Because of) Christ's stay in the tomb...the same person of the 'Living One' can say, 'I died, and behold I am alive for evermore.' Since the 'Author of life' who was killed is the same 'living one (who has) risen,' the divine person of the Son of God necessarily continued to possess his human soul and body, separated from each other by death.

Christ's death was a real death in that it put an end to his earthly human existence. But because of the union which the person of the Son retained with his body, his was not a mortal corpse like others, for 'it was not possible for death to hold him...' Jesus' Resurrection 'on the third day' was a sign of this also because bodily decay was held to begin on the fourth day after death.

Baptism, the original and full sign of which is immersion, efficaciously signifies the descent into the tomb by the Christian who dies to sin with Christ in order to live a new life.

(Catechism of the Catholic Church,
Paragraphs 624-628)

On Holy Saturday, the Church **sits** with Mary as did the disciples in the upper room. The tabernacle is empty and its doors are open so that all can see the emptiness. Sacraments are not celebrated until baptisms and confirmations and holy communion at the Easter Vigil, except to meet the needs of the dying. It is often a somber but peaceful day, as in a garden.

96 THE PASSION IN THE GREAT STORY OF JESUS

ADDITIONAL QUESTIONS

1. Did I notice anything else in the scripture text?

2. Sometimes, unhealed relationships within a family
   show themselves in the process of burying a loved
   one. And sometimes, in the process a great deal
   of healing happens within a family.
   How do I think things were for the disciples
   who seem to not be a part of his burial?

3. Mark suggests a simple and stark burial,
   like one for a pauper.
   John gives a more honorable and regal burial.
   Which do I think is more historical?
   What is the theological meaning of the other?

4. In William Barclay's commentary on the pious act of
   Joseph of Arimathea, burying Jesus, though there is
   *no hint that he spoke one word in Jesus' favor or intervened
   in any way on his behalf* at the Sanhedrin trial, adds:

   > *It is one of the commonest tragedies of life that we keep
   > our wreaths for people's graves and our praises until they
   > are dead. It would be infinitely better to give them some
   > of these flowers and some of these words of gratitude
   > when they are still alive.* (Barclay)

   Are there any wreaths of gratitude I want to share?

BURIAL

97

CLOSING PRAYER

Are there intercessions from the group?

Continue with a portion of the song:
Stabat Mater
Text: Jacopone da Todi, *Stabat Mater dolorosa*, d. 1306,
translated by Edward Caswell, altered
Verse 3 by Stephen J. Wolf, 2011
Music: 88 7 STABAT MATER, *Mainz Gesanbbuch*, 1661

At the cross, her sta-tion keep-ing,
Stood the mourn-ful moth-er weep-ing,
Where he hung, the dy-ing Lord.

Saw him then from judge-ment ta-ken,
And in death by all for-sa-ken,
Till his Spir-it he re-signed.

Sit with her this Sab-bath Ho-ly
Let our time with her be whole-ly
Bless-ed in our grief to share.

Je-sus, may her deep de-vo-tion
Stir in me the same e-mo-tion,
Heart to heart ac-cep-tance find.

Hail Mary, full of grace, the Lord is with you.
Blessed are you among women,
and blessed is the fruit of your womb, Jesus.
Holy Mary, mother of God, pray for us now
and at the hour of our death. Amen.

SOURCES and FOR MORE

Scripture in the Comparative Texts is rendered for reflection
in the present tense by the editor.
**OPENING READINGS in group sessions should
be done from group members' personal study
bibles and not from the Comparative Texts.**

Kurt Aland, Editor, *Synopsis of the Four Gospels*
(English text Second Edition of the *Revised Standard
Version*), United Bible Societies, 1985.
This classic work was most helpful in organizing the
Comparative Texts.

*The NRSV-NIV Parallel New Testament in Greek and
English: With Interlinear Translation by Alfred Marshall,*
Zondervan Publishing House, 1990
This used used heavily in rendering the Comparative
Texts in the present tense.

Raymond E. Brown, S.S., Joseph A. Fitzmyer, S.J.,
Roland E. Murphy, O.Carm., Editors,
The New Jerome Biblical Commentary, 1990,especially
the articles by Harrington, Viviano, Karris and Perkins
mentioned below.

Raymond E. Brown, S.S. *The Death of the Messiah,* 2 Volumes,
Doubleday: Anchor Bible Reference Library, 1994.

- Brown, *The Passion Narratives of the Gospels,* a conference
now available on CD from **welcome recordings.com**.
The summaries on pages 14, 30-31, 48, 62, 78, and 90
And the drawing on page 72 are adapted from this.
This is my favorite of this scholar's recordings.

Footnotes of the *New American Bible, Revised Edition*, United
States Conference of Catholic Bishops (USCCB), 2010.
The NABRE footnotes are the best accessible concise
scripture commentary available.

THE PASSION IN THE GREAT STORY OF JESUS

Pheme Perkins, *Reading the New Testament*, 2nd Edition, Paulist Press, 1988.

Page 17: *To pray in the deepest...*; Robert Barron, (I have lost track of where I read this quote, though every search for it has been a great joy; it may be from class notes. My favorite of the books by this great teacher is) *The Strangest Way: Walking the Christian Path*, Orbis Books, 2002.

Page 17: *You feel you are hedged in...*; Gabriel Marcel, *Homo Viator: Introduction to a Metaphysic of Hope*, translated by Emma Craufurd, Gloucester: Peter Smith, 1978.

Page 17: *If you want peace, go to sleep. But if you want to be alive, go to prayer.* Buddhist monk **Geshe Sopa** speaking at Mundelein Seminary. Somebody in the crowd asked if prayer was the way to find peace. This was his answer.

Page 35: *I remember in Birmingham...*; Martin Luther King, Jr. in Memphis, Tennessee on April 3, 1968 in *Martin Luther King, Jr.: A Documentary... Montgomery to Memphis*, Published by W.W. Norton and Company

Page 40: *NOTE: 'Ioudaion - Judeans...*; John J. Pilch, *The Cultural Dictionary of the Bible*, The Liturgical Press, 1999.

Page 49: *To Pilate's credit...*; *The New World Dictionary Concordance to the New American Bible*, C.D. Stampley Enterprises, Inc., 1970, out of print.

Page 52: *Three Degrees of Humility*; Saint Ignatius of Loyola, *The Spiritual Exercises*, especially #165-168. The best way to experience the exercises is on an individually directed retreat. Find Jesuit retreat centers at www.jesuits.org/retreat-centers.

Page 63: *The crucifixion is told in...*; Daniel J. Harrington, S.J., "The Gospel According to Mark," *The New Jerome Biblical Commentary* (above), Prentice Hall, 1990, pp. 626-28;

THE PASSION IN THE GREAT STORY OF JESUS

Page 64: *If an innocent man...;**The Holy Bible, Revised Standard Version**, Second Catholic Edition, Ignatius Press, 2006, footnote to Luke 23:31.

Page 65: *When Harry Potter gave clothing (a sock) to Dobby the House Elf, he set him free.* **Harry Potter and the Chamber of Secrets**, 2002.

Page 65: *A slaves death on the cross...*; Benedict T. Viviano, O.P., "The Gospel According to Matthew," *The New Jerome Biblical Commentary*, Prentice Hall, 1990, pp.670-73;

Page 65: *The criminal has deep faith...*;Robert J. Karris, O.F.M., "The Gospel According to Luke," *The New Jerome Biblical Commentary* (above), Prentice Hall, 1990, pp. 717-20;

Page 66: *It is impossible to decide...*; Pheme Perkins, "The Gospel According to John," *The New Jerome Biblical Commentary* (above), Prentice Hall, 1990, pp. 979-82.

Page 66: *devotion to her is dangerous...*; Megan McKenna, **Mary Shadow of Grace**, Orbis Books, 1995, quoted in **A Sourcebook about Mary**, Liturgy Training Publications, 2002, pg. 100.

Page 68: *Forgiveness is hard...*; Daniel E Pilarczyk, **Lenten Luches: Reflections on the Weekday Readings for Lent and Easter Week**, St. Anthony Messenger Press, 1995.

Page 69:...*cannot forgive up to four...* ; Martin Luther King, Jr., quote from **A Reconciliation Sourcebook**, edited by Kathleen Hughes and Joseph A. Favazza, Liturgy Training Publications, 1997, pg. 91

Page 84: *The Good Friday Reproaches*; **The Roman Missal:** *English Translation According to the Third Typical Edition,* United States Conference of Catholic Bishops (USCCB), 2010.

Page 91: *Just as Jesus shared with us the experience of a mother's womb, so he shares with humanity the experience of a grave*; Having lost the source of this phrase of truth, I still search.

SOURCES AND FOR MORE 101

Pages 94-95: *In his plan of salvation...*; **Catechism of the Catholic Church**, United States Conference of Catholic Bishops (USCCB), Liguori Publications, 1997.

Page 96:*...no hint that he spoke one word...*; William Barclay, **The Gospel of Mark**, Westminster John Knox Press, 1975, revised 2001. Barclay's readable *Daily Study Bible* is full of great stories, images and insights.

The Passion in the Great Story of Jesus

is the 9th short faith-sharing book
(ninety minutes once a week over six weeks)
by parish priest Stephen Joseph Wolf

PONDERING Our FAITH: revised with the new creed
1. The New Evangelization: revelation, faith, the trinity...
2. The Church: discipleship, community, family, prayer...
3. Sacraments: baptism, confirmation, eucharist, healing...
4. Vocation: holy orders, marriage, human dignity...
5. Moral Formation in Christ: grace, virtue, conscience...
6. The Sacred: liturgical year, art, music, devotions...

TREE of LIFE: Saint Bonaventure on the Christ Story
Based on the Twelve Fruits of the *Tree of Life*.
The Mystery of the Incarnation
1. 1st His Distinguished Origin; 2nd His Humble Way of Life
2. 3rd The Loft of his Power; 4th The Plenitude of his Piety
The Mystery of his Passion
3. 5th Confidence in Trials; 6th Patience in Bad Treatment
4. 7th Constancy under Torture; 8th Victory in the Conflict
The Mystery of his Glory
5. 9th The Novelty of his Resurrection; 10th The Ascension
6. 11th The Equity of his Judgment; 12th Eternal Kingdom

THE PASSION IN THE GREAT STORY OF JESUS

FORTY PENANCES for SPIRITUAL EXERCISE:
living the great gift of mercy

These "penances" are presented as spiritual exercises to continue the conversion experience that has already begun with the awareness that one has sinned, and are arranged following the Exercises of St. Ignatius of Loyola:

1. Reality of God's Complete Love
2. Reality of Sin and Reconciliation
3. Universal Call to Holiness   *seeds planted*
4. Vocation "Yes"   *memories provoked*
5. Perfect Act of Love   *questions raised*
6. Wholly New Way   *actions prompted*

GOD'S MONEY: where faith meets life in the world

Through 14 tax seasons, Stephen Joseph Wolf became a certified public accountant and an accredited personal financial specialist before entering seminary. These six chapters draw heavily from the experience of those years.

1. Micah's Vine & Fig Tree
2. Daily Bread This Day
3. Building a Bigger Barn
4. Parables of Stewards   *Everything*
5. When Life is Changed   *belongs to God*
6. Community of Believers   See Deut. 10:14

BEING SPOUSES: from celibate observation

Unable to find a healthy parish resource about what marriage is, the author wrote this well-received work.

1. Marriage Sacramentality
2. The Domestic Church
3. Permanence
4. Fidelity   from one of my
5. Children   married brothers:
6. Intimacy   *You can't know.*

MORE BY STEPHEN JOSEPH WOLF

TWELVE-STEP SPIRITUALITY for CHRISTIANS
following Vernon J. Bittner's *Twelve Steps for Christian Living*
Here is a helpful introduction to this spirituality
for those who may be unfamiliar with it.

1. When I Am Weak
2. Let Go and Let God
3. Sick As Our Secrets
4. Progress, Not Perfection   *because everyone*
5. Let It Begin With Me   *is addicted*
6. One Day At A Time   *to something*

ANGER the JESUS WAY: *reflections on*
the only gospel story where the author said Jesus was angry,
the healing of a man with a withered hand in Mark 3:1-6

1. The Story
2. Watched in the Sabbath Assembly
3. Invited by Jesus
4. Riddle Silence   *Looking around at them*
5. Anger-Grief   *with anger and grieved...*
6. Turning to Freedom   Mark 3:5

PLANNING MY OWN FUNERAL?
a four-week way to pray it

1. Vigil
2. Readings
3. Eucharist   *surprised we laughed*
4. Left Behind   *so much...*

Some of the PRAYERBOOKS
by STEPHEN JOSEPH WOLF

Hinge Hours for Ordinary Time (& companion volumes for the seasons)
One Week in Ordinary Time   *In Health & In Healing*
A Jesus Breviary   *31 Days of God's Love-Call*
Gone Before Us: praying for the dead   idjc.org

CPSIA information can be obtained
at www.ICGtesting.com
Printed in the USA
LVOW12s0528110217
523685LV00002B/2/P